Retirement Planning That Delivers

5 Powerful Strategies for Your Best Bucket-List Results, a Longer Healthspan, and More Memorable Experiences

Pete Bosse, PhD, CFP®

DEDICATION

This book is dedicated to and was inspired by my parents, Al and Lorraine Bosse, my wife Helen, and the numerous veterans I have worked with over the last few years. I especially want to thank my editor, Wendy Brzezinski, for making me a better writer.

CONTENTS

PREFACE

JOHN LENNON

I AM GRATEFUL TO BE ALIVE! I cherish every remaining day I have on this planet. You see, I was diagnosed with cancer in 2023, and I've been in a battle. I'm not yet sure who is going to win this fight. My first grandfather died at age 67 when I was only three years old. My second grandfather died at age 60 when I was 15 years old. None of us know how long we have to live. Now, at age 64 and retired for the third time, I am planning, prioritizing, and doing only those things that bring me true joy and happiness.

There are a lot of books out there about retirement and financial planning. This book is different because it focuses on identifying what you want from retirement and how to get it. This book is

---

1. https://quotefancy.com/quote/27855/John-Lennon-Life-is-very-short-and-there-s-no-time-for-fussing-and-fighting-my-friends , accessed on 9/19/24.

designed to help you maximize your retirement joy and minimize your regrets at death. As a CERTIFIED FINANCIAL PLANNER ® Professional, I'd like to tell you retirement is about much more than a number, whether that number is your age or your retirement nest egg. Retirement is about spending your remaining time and attention doing what's important to you. But without clarity of purpose and goals, how can you possibly know what you will need in retirement? For example, if you wanted to spend 100% of your retired time fishing or doing volunteer work and giving back to your community, you would likely not require as many resources as someone who wanted to buy a vacation home on a lake and also travel the world for the remainder of their time. Do you see the difference?

In his book *The Art of the Good Life*, Rolf Dobelli notes that you won't find happiness in status, expensive cars, your bank account, or social success. Happiness can be found only in your mental fortress. Noted psychologist Viktor Frankl defines *mental fortress* as the last of human freedoms, which is to choose one's attitude to things.[2]

Suppose you are seeking the key to retirement happiness. In that case, a book called *The Good Life* discusses the results of this 84-year Harvard study of happiness, indicating that the key is good relationships, which keep us healthier and happier. Period.[3]

---

2. Dobelli, R. (2017). *The art of the good life: 52 surprising shortcuts to happiness, wealth, and success*. Hachette Books.
3. Waldinger, R., & Schulz, M. (2023). *The good life*. New York, NY: Simon & Schuster.

Quick Tip:

"There isn't time, so brief is life, for bickerings, apologies, heart-burnings, callings to account. There is only time for loving, and but an instant, so to speak, for that." [4]

MARK TWAIN

If you're aged 50+, the book you are holding is for you! Retirement can be a two-edged sword: it can be exciting and simultaneously worrisome. Maybe you're excited to be on your own time clock yet fearful of runaway inflation, Social Security instability, rising Medicare costs, an unpredictable stock market, and maintaining your health as you age. You're excited about traveling and spending time with the grandkids but concerned about taxes or just frustrated with a constant barrage of email scams and annoying telemarketers targeting retirees. You may be exhausted from travel battles with airlines, rental car agencies, and hotels, where 'service' has gone entirely out of 'customer service.' Or, perhaps, you feel that no matter how hard you try, you're always on the wrong side of the outcome.

If you let life's ups and downs get the best of you, you may become depressed and unhappy with life in general. Your relationships may suffer, and you may get so upset that you want to punch holes in the wall. Furthermore, you may need to make better decisions without relying on wrong information that could cost you thousands of dollars. Worse yet, if you maintain this ravenous cycle, you may quickly spiral down six feet underground and only briefly enjoy the retirement you have worked so hard to achieve!

---

4. Waldinger, R., & Schulz, M. (2023). *The good life*. New York, NY: Simon & Schuster.

I served in various roles with the U.S. Army from 1980 to 2020, so you may see some colorful phrases, quotations, and anecdotes sprinkled throughout this book along with *Quick Tips,* such as *"When you have exhausted all possibilities, remember this: you haven't."* —Thomas A. Edison.

This book is crafted to challenge the conventional narratives of retirement planning. It's centered on something other than how much you need to save or the best investments for your pension. Instead, it's about enriching the years you've earned with health, happiness, and a lasting legacy. We will explore five powerful strategies, with each chapter designed to be reflective and action-able, providing you with the tools to build a retirement that is as rewarding as it is secure.

The tone of this book will be conversational and motivational, mirroring the discussions I've had with many individuals approaching their retirement years. It's intended for you, the reader, to feel you're receiving advice from a trusted friend with decades of experience in both the battlefield and the boardroom.

I've structured the book to ease you into each topic, starting with relatable examples and moving into practical, actionable strategies. These stories will inspire and guide you - from the veteran who rediscovered his zeal for life through community service to the executive who found new joy in pursuing health and wellness adventures.

The importance of starting your retirement planning now cannot be overstated. Whether you're in the early stages of your career contemplation or a few years into retirement, it's never too late—or too early—to refine your approach to these crucial years. I will show you why a well-rounded plan is necessary and how it can significantly enhance your life post-career through statistics, personal anecdotes, and proven strategies. Hundreds of research papers show humans have an innate drive to be autonomous, self-determined, and connected. When that drive is liberated, people achieve more and live richer lives.[5]

I invite you to dive into this journey with an open mind and an eager heart. Engage with the exercises, reflect on the checklists, and personalize the insights to fit your unique situation. This book isn't just about reading; it's about doing, about transforming theoretical knowledge into practical, life-enhancing actions. I'll always encourage you to dream about your retirement life and not be afraid to dream big.

As we embark on this journey together, I hope you will find guidance and inspiration in these pages to help you forge a retirement filled with joy, purpose, and satisfaction. Your best retired life awaits—more prosperous and attainable than you might think. Let's start building it together! Pete Bosse

---

5. Pink, D. H. (2011). *Drive*. Canongate Books.

INTRODUCTION

"Drench yourself in words unspoken,

Live your life with arms wide open,

Today is where your book begins,

The rest is still unwritten." [1]

NATASHA BEDINGFIELD

Just 4% of retirees say they are "living the dream," based on a recent survey by an asset management company.[2] John had always thought he was ready for retirement. A meticulous planner, his finances were in impeccable order. But three years into what should have been his golden era, he found himself grappling with a nagging sense of purposelessness and declining health. This was not the retirement he had envisioned. His story isn't unique, and it

1. https://ffm.to/unwrittenacoustic , accessed on 9/20/24.
2. https://www.cnbc.com/2024/05/09/4percent-of-current-retirees-say-they-are-living-the-dream-survey-finds.html , accessed on 9/18/24.

underscores a profound truth: successful retirement is not just about financial preparedness; it's about well-being across every aspect of life.

My name is Pete Bosse, and I'm living a joyful retired life despite significant adversity.

That adversity included a gut-wrenching $100,000 divorce, a surprising 13-month military deployment to Iraq, the loss of $2 million in the 2009 stock market crash, and a recent cancer diagnosis in 2023. Yet I've reached most of my life goals, including retiring from the corporate world at age 45, completing my PhD at age 50, retiring from the military at age 59, passing the CFP® Professional exam at 62, and retiring from my third act as a government employee at age 63! Now, at age 64, I'm publishing this book.

My journey has taken me from the strategic operations of Fortune 100 companies to the disciplined ranks of the military, where I retired as a Major General. Beyond these roles, I've dedicated substantial time to helping heroes in Homes For Our Troops and veterans in the Coordinated Assistance Network find their footing in civilian life. With a PhD in Business Administration and certification in financial planning, I've learned that retirement planning, much like military strategy, requires a comprehensive approach that considers all facets of life.

Quick Tip:

"Courage isn't having the strength to go on; it is going on when you don't have strength."

NAPOLEON BONAPARTE

My retirement story is about resilience—the ability to bounce back from adversity by incorporating positive psychology, financial preparation, and retirement planning principles—and finding joy, passion, and purpose in creating my dream retirement.

This book is different. It's not about your retirement number, portfolio size, or the many things you have. It's about the softer side of retirement. <u>This book is designed to help you maximize your retirement joy and minimize your regrets at death.</u> I've organized this book around five powerful strategies for retirement: Extending Healthspan, Finding Purpose, Creating Experiences, Building Resilience, and Financial Security. Below, in Figure 1, is what I call the Max. Retired Life Model. It focuses on these five powerful retirement strategies, using a bullseye starting from the inside and moving out, with 80% focused on you and what you want and 20% on where and how to fund what you want.

Figure 1. Max. Retired Life Model

This book will focus on five powerful strategies to help you live your best retired life. This book will start in the middle of the Figure 1 bullseye with Strategy 1, Extending Healthspan, and identifying strategies for maintaining, stabilizing, and lengthening it so that you may remain active well into retirement. Healthspan is how long you stay healthy enough to do what you want. Everything starts with you and taking care of yourself. The downhill slide cannot be reversed once your body and mind begin to atrophy. Therefore, staying physically and mentally fit as long as possible is imperative.

Strategy 2: In the next ring from the Figure 1 bullseye, you will discover purpose, passions, meaning, and goals. The aim is to concentrate on what truly matters to you—not what society, family, or advertisements dictate, but *your* personal passions that bring you excitement, joy, and fulfillment.

Next, in Strategy 3, we'll explore creating the memorable experiences that will form your fondest memories of your retired years. Possible bucket-list examples include travel, spending time with family and friends, building relationships, volunteering, learning a new language, returning to school, pursuing a hobby, or starting a side hustle.

Then, in Strategy 4, we'll discuss building resilience and how to bounce back from adversity. No matter how much you've planned, you'll likely get knocked down at some point. It could be the death of a close friend or spouse, a 30% drop in the stock market, a tornado that destroys your home, a late-life divorce, or a fire that ravages your church. We'll explore tools to help you bounce back and recover.

Finally, in Strategy 5, we will move on to financial security only after we've spent 80% of the time on you and what you want. We'll discuss income and expenses, supporting your needs and the needs of others, your legacy, and dying with zero remaining resources. One school of thought centers on experiences versus things and trying to maximize your experiences and memories.[3] To do that, you must spend while you can.

> *Quick Tip: All the money in the world couldn't help a 56-year-old billionaire with pancreatic cancer (e.g., Steve Jobs) buy more time and create more family memories. So, how much money is enough to do what you want? It would be best if you did these things while you still can. Timing is everything.*

According to a 2024 Prudential survey, fifty-five-year-old Americans are far less financially secure than older generations, and they face mental and emotional strain that goes beyond the standard "mid-life" crisis.[4] Moreover, research on lottery winners[5] indicates sudden financial fortune does not improve happiness. The study results confirm the old wisdom that it is not what happens to a person that determines the quality of life but what a person makes happen.[6] I know miserable rich people. I also know people with absolutely nothing who are incredibly happy. Money is not the answer.

---

3. Perkins, B. J. (2020). *Die with zero: Getting all you can from your money and your life.* Boston, MA: Houghton Mifflin.
4. https://news.prudential.com/latest-news/prudential-news/prudential-news-details/2024/2024-Pulse-of-the-American-Retiree-Survey/default.aspx , accessed on 8/25/24.
5. Brickman, P., Coates, D., & Janoff-Bulman, R. (1978). Lottery winners and accident victims: Is happiness relative? *Journal of Personality and Social Psychology,* 36(8), 917–927. https://doi.org/10.1037/0022-3514.36.8.917, accessed 9/29/24.
6. Brickman, P. D., Coates, D., & Janoff-Bulman, R. (1978). Lottery winners and accident victims: Is happiness relative. *Journal of Personality and Social Psychology,* 36(8), 917–927.

Time is NOT on your side. Remember when you were young and watched sand flowing through an hourglass? It was slow and hardly seemed to move at all. Now, later in life, that same sand appears to have picked up speed and is rapidly nearing its end. You do NOT want to reach the end of your life and have regrets. In her bestselling book, *The Top Five Regrets of the Dying*, Bronnie Ware summarizes her learning from 20-plus years of hospice care into this advice to live your life with no regrets: "Be who you are, find balance, speak honestly, value those you love, and allow yourself to be happy."[7]

Over the last ten years, I've learned much about retirement, and I will share personal examples, stories, anecdotes, exciting vignettes, *Quick Tips*, and real-life examples to drive home each point.

I've learned there are three overarching phases of retirement. Each phase can vary based on your health, desires, and goals.

- Phase 1 is the **Go-Go phase**, where you enjoy your newly discovered free time. You want to travel, spend time with friends and family, perhaps golf daily, or do things you've been waiting decades to do. The luster of this phase fades with time and may last 1-3 years.
- Phase 2, the **Slow-Go phase**, is when you start getting bored with all that excitement and seek purpose and meaning in your retired time. This is the most prolonged phase and truly sets you up to accomplish those things that are important to you while you still can in the time you have remaining.
- Phase 3 is the **No-Go phase**, where your failing health prevents you from doing your desired things. This is why

---

7. Ware, B. (2019). *The top five regrets of the dying*. USA: Hay House, Inc.

it is vitally essential that you sequence your experiences and plans to match your phase of retirement. It should be front-loaded because, at some undeterminable point, you won't be able to climb Mount Everest, jump from a plane, walk the Great Wall of China, or travel by plane to see your grandchildren.

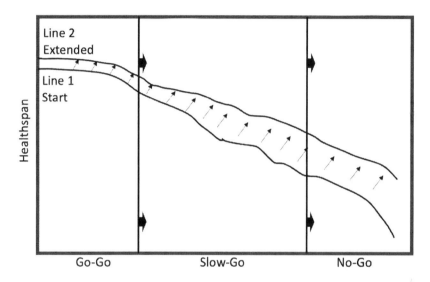

Figure 2. Retirement Phases

If Line 1 of Figure 2 is the average Healthspan at the start of your retirement journey, then you want to do activities and develop habits that can extend your Healthspan to Line 2. This will increase the duration of your Healthspan and extend your enjoyable time in Phase 1 and Phase 2 since you can do more activities that you otherwise might be unable to accomplish. Your biggest fear ought to be wasting your life and time, not 'Am I going to have X number of dollars when I'm 80?'[8]

---

8. Perkins, B. J. (2020). *Die with zero: Getting all you can from your money and your life*. Boston, MA: Houghton Mifflin.

Please join me on this journey to extend your Healthspan, discover your purpose, create memorable experiences, fund your prioritized goals, and build the resilience to withstand the roughest retirement storms. Ultimately, I want you to design and enjoy the retirement of your dreams!

STRATEGY 1-
EXTENDING HEALTHSPAN
PRESERVATION AND DURATION

"If you retreat, or if you retire or withdraw from life, your capacities will slowly regress."

DR. MICHAEL MERZENICH

I observed my mother's health rapidly decline over the last five years of her life due to lack of exercise, poor nutritional habits, and the growing impact of chronic illness. Contrast that to my 85-year-old father, who walks 2-3 miles daily, watches what he eats, and engages actively with his church and community. He remains very healthy and active today. Everything starts with you and taking care of yourself. In his international best-selling book, *The 7 Habits of Highly Effective People*, Dr. Stephen R. Covey talks about Habit 7: Sharpening the Saw.[1] His Habit 7 focuses on you and the four areas of balanced self-renewal: physical, mental, social/emotional, and spiritual.

---

1. Covey, S. R. (1989). *The seven habits of highly effective people: Restoring the character ethic*. New York, NY: Simon & Schuster.

Similarly, our Strategy 1 will focus on maximizing your healthspan and extending it so that you may remain active and engaged for as long as possible. Healthspan is how long you stay physically and mentally healthy enough to do what you want. Our lives consist of many habits. The good habits help preserve and maintain your health for as long as possible, while the bad habits may expedite its atrophy.

> *Quick Tip – Some say sitting is the new smoking. So, get up and move to live longer.*

One year ago, I started walking in our neighborhood every morning. It's about a 2-mile walk. Gradually, I added two 5-pound weights, then a 10-pound weighted vest, and recently, I've moved up to 10-pound weights that I carry while I walk. Over the last year, I've lost 20 pounds, and I am also focusing on better nutrition and reduced intake of sugar and carbohydrates. Nearly every morning, about halfway through my walk, I see a gentleman sitting on a folding chair in his garage with the door wide open. He smokes a cigarette daily and does something on his mobile phone.

So, let me ask you: which is the good habit and which is the bad habit? Which habit above is more likely to prolong your healthspan, and which is more likely to cut it short? I'm not being judgmental; I'm merely observing the facts and their potential outcomes based on current medical science. Let's explore steps to extend your healthspan, giving you more time to do what you want.

When Ellen turned 65, she celebrated her retirement, eager for the long-awaited freedom it promised. Fast forward five years, Ellen grappled with unexpected health challenges that sidelined her plans for travel and leisure. Her realization? Health is indeed wealth, especially in retirement. This pivotal moment led Ellen to shift her focus towards maintaining and enhancing her health, ensuring her later years remained vibrant and fulfilling. Her story is a powerful reminder for all of us: managing our healthspan—our time of good health—is crucial to avoiding illness and enjoying our retirement to the fullest.

Let's transform your golden years by emphasizing health preservation and duration. It's about creating a lifestyle that extends your life and enriches it with vitality and vigor. Here, you'll discover practical strategies and insights that focus on maintaining your physical well-being through fitness, ensuring you have the energy and strength to enjoy every moment of your retirement. As Marie Forleo, author of *Everything is Figureoutable*, reminds us, You are 100 percent responsible for your life.[2]

1.1 FITNESS AFTER FIFTY: STAYING ACTIVE FOR LONG-TERM HEALTH

Advantages of Regular Exercise

Staying physically active is more than just a choice. It's necessary to stay healthy as you age. Movement helps maintain your strength, keeps your joints flexible, and improves your balance, reducing the risk of falls, a big concern as people age. Additionally, exercise has a significant impact on brain function. Research shows that engaging in activity can significantly reduce the chances of cognitive decline and diseases like Alzheimer's. The beauty of exercise lies in its benefits—it benefits your body and

---

2. Forleo, M. (2019). *Everything is figureoutable*. USA: Penguin Random House LLC.

rejuvenates your mind, keeping you alert and involved. So, rest assured, you're making the right choice for your health by staying active. We'll introduce the subject here and then go into additional detail about building resilience in Chapter 4.

Customized Workout Plans

Not every exercise plan suits everyone, especially as you grow older. The key is personalization. For example, if arthritis concerns you, water aerobics can offer a workout without straining your joints. Resistance training could benefit individuals with osteoporosis as it helps strengthen bones and improve balance. Programs such as Tai Chi are ideal for enhancing balance and promoting calmness. Your fitness routine should consider your history, current health condition, and, importantly, what activities you enjoy. Ultimately, the effective workout is one that you stick to because you genuinely appreciate it.

Incorporating Routine

Incorporating exercise into your schedule doesn't have to be a hassle or require lifestyle alterations. Start by building on what you enjoy doing. For example, if you appreciate morning strolls (like me), think about picking up the pace or exploring paths with some inclines to enhance your workout. Try the stairs instead of the elevator. Try parking farther from the store entrance. These simple adjustments can significantly boost your physical activity level without overwhelming you.

> *Quick Tip: Two years ago, I switched from sitting at a desk to using a standing desk. Initially, it was a bit challenging. It took me around 60 days to get used to the changes. My*

*back pain has gone today, and my core feels more vital than
ever.*

It's vital to prioritize consistency over intensity when you begin.
Focus on establishing a routine more than striving for perfection.
Always remember that the aim is to improve your life, not compli-
cate it. A 2022 study found that even brief 1-2 minute bursts of
intermittent exercise 3 times daily lowered the risk of death by 38-
40%.[3] That reminds me of a drill sergeant I had in basic training
and the harsh advice he had every day for all the Privates, myself
included, "Get up and move your goat-smelling a**es now."

Safety First

Exercising is crucial for your well-being, especially as you get
older. Starting with a warm-up, like a walk, is essential to prepare
your muscles and prevent injuries. Likewise, remember to cool
down after each workout by stretching. Staying hydrated is vital,
so drink water during and after your workouts. Listen to your
body. Know your limits. The aim of exercising as you age isn't
competing or breaking records; it's about maintaining and
enhancing your health and overall quality of life.

By following these tips, you can make exercise an enjoyable and
lasting part of your retirement routine, helping you stay active and
full of vitality.

---

3. Stamatakis, E., Ahmadi, M. N., Gill, J. M. R., et al. (2022). Association of wearable device-measured vigorous intermittent lifestyle physical activity with mortality. *Nature Medicine, 28,* 2521–2529. https://doi.org/10.1038/s41591-022-02100-
x , accessed on 8/15/24.

1.2 NUTRITION OVERHAUL: EATING WELL IN YOUR GOLDEN YEARS

As we grow older, our bodies go through changes. Our nutritional requirements shift accordingly. It's not about eating less; it's about providing our bodies with nutrients that cater to a slower metabolism and alterations in body structure. For individuals, preserving muscle mass, maintaining bone strength, and increasing energy levels become vital, and our food choices can impact these aspects. A diet that includes calcium, vitamin D, fiber, and essential proteins while limiting saturated fats and empty calories can significantly benefit our well-being by helping prevent age-related conditions like osteoporosis and heart disease.

The secret to maintaining a diet in your golden years isn't strict limitations; it's about making intelligent swaps and finding balance. For example, swapping out meat for fish such as salmon or mackerel can increase your omega-3 fatty acid intake, which is crucial in maintaining heart health and reducing inflammation. Choosing grains ensures a consistent fiber supply that aids digestion and helps regulate blood sugar levels. These gradual but steady adjustments contribute to improved health and heightened energy levels, allowing you to enjoy your activities fully.

> *Quick Tip: Over a decade ago, I switched from white bread to 12-grain bread, and now I can't even stand the taste of white bread. I love my 12-grain bread for breakfast toast, and it's much healthier than white bread.*

Knowing how to interpret food labels is a skill that empowers you to make good food choices. Food labels may appear confusing to many with all their percentages and measurements. However, once you decode them, they offer insights into the content of the food you're about to eat. Paying attention to elements like sodium—keeping it low —and dietary fiber—which should be high—can significantly impact the effectiveness of your diet. Select labels that prioritize foods as ingredients and steer clear of lengthy lists of additives—a handy guideline that simplifies grocery shopping and enhances overall health.

Where can you discover nutritious and suitable recipes for seniors? Resources tailored explicitly for adults offer ideas for nutrient-rich meals that are easy to prepare and cater to various dietary needs and preferences. Websites such as the National Institute on Aging present many recipes to meet seniors' unique needs. Additionally, magazines dedicated to healthy aging serve as sources of culinary inspiration.

Many guides provide meal plans that consider energy requirements, challenges with chewing or swallowing, and ways to enhance interaction during meals, which are just as crucial for mental well-being as the nutritional aspect is for physical health.

> *Quick Tip: Some studies suggest intermittent fasting or restricting food consumption to an 8-hour period could positively affect heart health, memory retention, and diabetes prevention.*

In essence, adjusting your diet as you get older isn't about giving up the pleasures of eating but about making wiser choices to improve your well-being and vitality. By focusing on food nutrients, understanding food labels better, and utilizing tailored resources for seniors, you can significantly elevate your quality of life in retirement. This comprehensive approach to nutrition sets the stage for a vibrant phase of life where each meal enriches your body and spirit.

Quick Tip: Our aunt is 96 years old and lives in Florida. She likes a Budweiser beer now and then and also likes grocery store ice cream by the quart. At her age, she can do whatever she wants! But I need to worry about my next 30 years of eating.

1.3 MENTAL: ENRICHING YOUR COGNITIVE LANDSCAPE

Like our bodies, our minds also require exercise and proper nourishment to stay healthy and active. As we grow older, it becomes crucial to keep our sharpness intact, not as a nice-to-have but as a necessity for preserving independence, nurturing personal connections, and enhancing overall well-being. Engaging in activities that challenge the mind and adopting habits that promote wellness are steps in maintaining brain vitality and improving cognitive functions such as memory, problem-solving, and flexibility of thought.

Boosting Brain Health Through Cognitive Exercises

Cognitive exercises involve participating in activities aimed at enhancing mental functions. For example, solving puzzles like crosswords or Sudoku can stimulate the brain and improve problem-solving capabilities and attention to detail. Similarly, learning a language or musical instrument can benefit by activating different brain regions and forming new neural pathways. These endeavors keep the mind active, which can help delay the decline often linked with aging. Each cognitive challenge is akin to a workout session for the brain—a practice for agility and strength.

Quick Tip: My wife enjoys playing Wordle with her siblings, while I am engrossed in Wordscapes on my smart-phone. Both games serve as fun tools to keep our minds alert and engaged. Stick with the free apps; they offer just as many mental challenges as the paid apps.

The Significance of Social Connections

'No road is long with good company' [4] – Turkish Proverb. Maintaining a vibrant social life plays a pivotal role in mental well-being. Social interactions help ward off depression and cognitive decline by providing emotional support, reducing stress, and encouraging a sense of belonging and purpose. Engaging regularly with friends, family, and community groups keeps your mind active and your spirits high. Whether joining a book club, attending community education classes, connecting with a spiritual organization, or simply sharing regular meals with friends, each social activity contributes to a healthier, more resilient mental state. Remember, loneliness and isolation can be as harmful to your mental health as physical inactivity is to your body; thus, staying socially active is imperative. An 85-year Harvard study on happiness found people who thrive the best in retirement find ways to cultivate connections.[5] A driver of loneliness is the absence of social connections, and loneliness is associated with a

4.   Kaufman, T., & Hiland, B. (2021). *Retiring? Your next chapter is about much more than money.* USA: Houndstooth Press.

5.   CNBC. (2023, March 10). 85-year Harvard happiness study found the biggest downside of retirement that no one talks about. Retrieved from https://www.cnbc.com/2023/03/10/85-year-harvard-happiness-study-found-the-biggest-downside-of-retirement-that-no-one-talks-about.html , accessed on 8/20/24.

greater risk of cardiovascular disease, dementia, stroke, depression, anxiety, and premature death.[6]

> *Quick Tip: Coincidentally, my 85-year-old father stays actively engaged in his church by volunteering to cook meals every Wednesday with fellow volunteers as a fundraiser. My wife and I like to meet friends at different restaurants every few months to catch up and try something new.*

Mindfulness and Meditation Practices

Mindfulness and meditation practices offer tools for improving clarity and emotional well-being by focusing on the present moment without judgment. Engaging in these practices regularly can help reduce stress levels, alleviate anxiety symptoms, combat depression, and enhance decision-making skills through thinking. Meditation has proven benefits, like improving focus, reducing work-related stress, and boosting well-being. You can easily incorporate these practices into your schedule by setting aside a few minutes each morning or evening for reflection or guided meditation, which creates a peaceful escape from the hustle and bustle of life.

Spirituality

As Karen Armstrong proclaims in her book, *A History of God*, "My study of the history of religion has revealed that human

---

6. Casey, H., (2024). Overcoming Loneliness in Retirement, NARFE Magazine, Vol. 100, Number 8.

beings are spiritual animals."[7] How do you address your spiritual needs? Spirituality can significantly boost resilience during retirement years marked by life changes. Engaging in activities like religion, mindfulness practices, or personal reflection lays the groundwork for inner strength and emotional balance. By finding a purpose or seeking meaning beyond possessions, individuals find it easier to handle the uncertainties and difficulties of retirement.

Quick Tip:

"Teach us to number our days and recognize how few they are; help us to spend them as we should."

PSALM 90:12 TLB

Embracing spirituality can bring a sense of calm and openness for retirees facing change gracefully by encouraging mindfulness and self-reflection to handle stress in the moment. Participating in activities like meditation or being part of a community can provide a network of support that lessens feelings of isolation and boosts health.

Spirituality also promotes a perspective on life and fosters feelings of hope and appreciation in retirees, enabling them to deal with difficulties effectively and see obstacles as opportunities for personal development. Ultimately, spirituality offers a sense of meaning and belonging, empowering retirees to stay strong amidst life changes.

---

7. Armstrong, K., (1993) A History of God, The 4,000-Year Quest of Judaism, Christianity and Islam, USA

Educational Pursuits: Keeping the Mind Engaged

Continual learning is another cornerstone of cognitive health. The adage 'use it or lose it' holds particularly true regarding brain function. Engaging in educational activities such as online courses, local workshops, or even travel can stimulate intellectual curiosity and cognitive engagement. Many universities and colleges offer classes designed for senior learners, providing education and valuable social interactions. Pursuing new knowledge keeps the brain active and engaged, provides a sense of achievement, and helps maintain cognitive functions. Whether history, science, art, or technology, every subject offers an opportunity to expand your horizons and challenge your mind.

> *Quick Tip: I pursued my CFP® Professional certification over 18 months and was thoroughly challenged by the coursework and the 6-hour certification exam.*

Integrating these exercises into your routine can be a manageable change. It begins with consistent actions: solving a crossword puzzle while sipping your morning coffee, joining a book club meeting every month, practicing meditation before bedtime, or enrolling in a course that intrigues you. Engaging in these activities strengthens your abilities, ensuring that your mind stays sharp and alert, as does your physical health. This comprehensive approach to well-being goes beyond preventing deterioration; it's about flourishing, evolving, and embracing life with wisdom gained through the years.

1.4 PREVENTATIVE: SAFEGUARDING YOUR HEALTH WITH PROACTIVE MEASURES

The essence of a fulfilling retirement is not just about enjoying the leisurely pace of life but also about ensuring you have the health to savor every moment. Proactive healthcare plays a pivotal role in this regard, focusing on prevention rather than cure. Health check-ups, effective management of conditions, keeping up with vaccinations, and routine examinations are the foundation of preventive care. They help you steer clear of health issues and make the most of your retirement years with peace of mind.

Essential Health Screenings

Regular health screenings protect against health problems that could impact your well-being. These screenings are crucial as they detect issues before symptoms surface, enabling intervention and better treatment outcomes. For example, colonoscopies, recommended every decade from age 50 onwards, can identify cancer in its early stages when treatment is most effective. Women are encouraged to undergo mammograms every one to two years, starting at age 50, to screen for breast cancer, while men may consider prostate exams for prostate health monitoring. Remember that these screening frequencies are recommendations; your doctor may advise a schedule based on your health background.

> *Quick Tip: I recently learned that Military Veterans are twice as likely as the general population to be diagnosed with prostate cancer.[8] Men, please watch your PSA and get*

---

8. https://zerocancer.org/help-and-support/resources-for/veterans

screened. My early cancer detection has opened up more possible treatment options.

Monitoring Chronic Conditions

Keeping track of conditions is essential as we grow older. Health issues like high blood pressure, diabetes, and arthritis are common. They can often be effectively managed with the right approach, preventing them from taking over your life. Regular monitoring and sticking to prescribed treatments are required. For example, controlling blood pressure can help prevent complications like heart disease and stroke. Managing blood sugar levels well can avoid diabetes-related problems such as nerve damage and kidney disease. Lifestyle changes like dieting and staying active are crucial, too; they can boost the effectiveness of medications. It's also essential to talk with your healthcare provider about any changes in your condition or how you're responding to treatment so that adjustments can be made accordingly.

Vaccination Importance

Our immune system becomes weaker as we age, making us more vulnerable to infections. Vaccinations play a role in healthcare. Seniors are advised to get annual flu shots; the shingles vaccine can help prevent a more prevalent condition in older individuals. Getting vaccinations is also recommended to shield against pneumonia, which is a significant cause of death among seniors. These vaccines offer a powerful way to enhance your immunity, guarding against illnesses that could significantly impact your well-being and mobility. They are an investment in a vibrant future where nothing hinders you from fully embracing life. Please consult your doctor before taking any vaccination.

Regular Check-Ups

Regular visits to your healthcare provider are about tackling problems and maintaining your overall health and wellness. These check-ups allow you and your doctor to review your health status, monitor ongoing conditions, and discuss any health concerns you might have. It's also a time to review your medications, supplements, and any other treatments you're undergoing. Consider these visits a tune-up for your body, ensuring everything runs smoothly, and any potential issues are caught early. They are an opportunity to discuss changes in your lifestyle, mental health, or physical condition, ensuring that your health strategy evolves with your needs. Regular interaction with your healthcare provider builds a relationship of trust and familiarity, which is invaluable as you navigate the complexities of health in your retirement years.

Proactive healthcare is about taking charge of your health and preventing disease before it starts. It's about regular screenings, managing chronic conditions, protecting against preventable diseases, and keeping close contact with your healthcare provider. This proactive approach ensures that you stay ahead of potential health issues, allowing you to focus more on enjoying your retirement versus constantly dealing with health issues.

1.5 SLEEP SCIENCE: TIPS FOR BETTER SLEEP IN RETIREMENT

Sleep's importance changes as we age, but its role remains crucial. Quality sleep is essential for health, especially as we age. It helps rejuvenate the body, strengthen memories, and repair muscles. However, our sleep patterns can shift during retirement, leading to lower-quality sleep. This shift can affect our energy levels and various aspects of health, from cognitive function to metabolic processes. Adapting to these changes is vital to enjoying a lifestyle in retirement.

Improving sleep habits is essential for sleep quality. It starts with creating a sleep environment. Your bedroom should be a place dedicated to rest. Please pay attention to your mattress and pillows, as they play a role in ensuring restful nights. Keep the room calm, cool, and serene to signal your body that it's time to unwind. Developing a consistent bedtime routine can also enhance sleep quality by signaling your body that it's time to wind down for the night through activities like reading or listening to calming music. Avoid looking at screens, such as TVs, phones, and computers, before going to bed, as the blue light they emit can disrupt the production of melatonin, which helps regulate our sleep patterns.

Many older adults are experiencing sleep problems like insomnia and sleep apnea. Insomnia makes it hard to fall and stay asleep, leading to tiredness and possibly worsening health issues. Sleep apnea, where breathing pauses occur during sleep, can cause health problems, such as heart disease and worsening memory problems, if not treated properly. Recognizing the signs of these conditions is essential. They may include waking up at night with loud snoring or feeling excessively tired during the day. If you notice any of these, it's important to see a healthcare provider who can suggest treatments like CPAP machines for sleep apnea or therapy for insomnia.

Quick Tip: I was diagnosed with sleep apnea about ten years ago, and I now use a CPAP mask every night—trust me, it works wonders. Before using CPAP treatment, I always felt sluggish and exhausted. Now, I wake up feeling refreshed and ready for the day. Getting accustomed to wearing a mask usually takes a couple of weeks to a month. After that, everything becomes more manageable.

Practicing relaxation techniques is key to improving sleep quality. Activities like meditation, deep breathing exercises, and gentle yoga can help relax the mind and prepare the body for sleep. Meditation, in particular, helps quiet one's thoughts and reduces stress, often hindering sleep. Deep breathing exercises enhance relaxation by boosting oxygen intake and lowering stress hormone levels, creating a state of sleep. Gentle yoga poses can be done in bed or near it to help release tension and soothe the system. Making these practices part of your bedtime routine can make a difference in how you sleep, allowing you to wake up feeling refreshed and ready for the day ahead.

Understanding the science behind sleep and adopting strategies to improve its quality becomes crucial as we navigate the challenges of aging. Establishing a sleeping environment, addressing any sleep disorders you may have, and using relaxation techniques can significantly enhance your sleep patterns and overall health and well-being. This comprehensive approach to managing sleep ensures your retirement years are fulfilling, vibrant, and enjoyable.

1.6 STRESS REDUCTION TECHNIQUES FOR A PEACEFUL LIFE

In the quiet moments of retirement, one would hope to find peace and experience a sense of calm relaxation naturally unfolding. Yet, for many, this new chapter brings its stressors. Whether it's adjusting to a slower pace of life, concerns about health and finances, or simply the challenge of filling one's days meaningfully, stress can manifest in myriad ways, subtly eroding the joy these years are meant to bring. Recognizing these stressors is the first step toward managing them effectively, ensuring they are manageable so you can enjoy this richly deserved time.

Identifying Stress Factors

Stress during retirement may manifest in many forms. It is not limited to worries like financial security or health concerns; it can also stem from minor daily obstacles accumulating over time. It could be the frustration of keeping up with evolving technology or the feeling of emptiness from missing one's work role and colleagues. It might involve meeting family expectations or maintaining a household for some individuals. Recognizing these experiences many retirees share can help alleviate some of the pressure. By pinpointing these stress factors, you can confront them directly rather than allowing them to linger beneath the surface and impact your physical well-being.

Effective Stress Management Techniques

Dealing with stress effectively involves using various techniques that can be adapted to situations and needs. Mindfulness, which consists of being fully present in the moment, is a way to combat stress. It teaches you to observe your thoughts and feelings without judgment, creating awareness that can help prevent stress from overwhelming you. In addition, by learning to pay attention to what's happening in front of us, we also increase our ability to act.[9] Journaling is another method that allows you to express and clarify your thoughts and emotions, providing an outlet for stress. Writing about your experiences and feelings as you transition into retire-

---

9. Waldinger, R., & Schulz, M. (2023). *The good life*. New York, NY: Simon & Schuster.

ment can be therapeutic, helping you navigate these changes positively. In addition, consider subtracting or stopping activities that don't provide joy or contribute to feeling overwhelmed. People who default to adding activities versus subtracting activities may miss opportunities to make their lives more fulfilling.[10]

Time management can seem less relevant in retirement, yet it remains a crucial skill. Without the structure of a full-time job, days can sometimes feel unanchored; managing your time well helps you stay active and engaged and carve out necessary periods for rest. Balancing activities and downtime is essential to preventing stress from becoming a constant presence. In addition, gratitude can make your life happier and more satisfying,[11] perhaps even less stressful, by inventorying what you are grateful for and then sharing it with those you care about.

Creating a Relaxing Environment

The environment in which you live plays a role in how you experience and handle stress. Establishing a peaceful and comforting space can significantly improve your ability to relax and unwind. Consider the layout and decoration of your home. Neglected areas can subtly contribute to feelings of unease or tension. Adjustments, like adding calming colors, ensuring natural light, or creating a unique space for relaxation—whether for reading, meditation, or enjoying music—can turn your home into a haven away from the pressures of the world outside.

---

10. Adams, G. S., Converse, B. A., Hales, A. H., & Klotz, L. E. (2021). People systematically overlook subtractive changes. *Nature, 592*(7853), 258-261. https://doi.org/10.1038/s41586-021-03380-y

11. Seligman, M. E. P. (2013). Flourish. Simon & Schuster.

Plants are beautiful and uplifting and have a proven effect on reducing stress and purifying the air. Similarly, the gentle sound of water from a small indoor fountain can be highly soothing and be a focal point for meditation or yoga practices. These elements can help create a serene atmosphere that supports stress reduction and promotes a sense of well-being.

When to Seek Help

Knowing when to seek assistance is crucial when stress becomes overwhelming. Signs that help may be necessary include feelings of sadness or depression, anxiety that disrupts daily life, or physical symptoms like insomnia, headaches, or loss of appetite. Consulting with a health expert can help you find tools to manage stress effectively. You'll then be able to develop personalized coping strategies based on your circumstances.

Furthermore, it's essential to recognize that seeking help is a display of strength rather than weakness. It demonstrates your dedication to self-care and your proactive efforts to maintain health. In some places where discussing health is still considered sensitive, speaking up and sharing your experiences can help inspire others to seek the support they need.

> Quick Tip: After my divorce, I sought counseling to help reduce stress and anxiety. One of the most powerful tips I learned was an encouragement from my therapist to "lean into the pain and feel it." His advice was to embrace the pain to get to the other side, and he was right—short-term pain for long-term gain. I had blocked out much of the pain, and now I can feel things again, and it's exciting and, also at times, scary.

To sum up, effectively handling stress enhances your retirement experience, allowing you to enjoy this phase of your life fully. You can protect your mental and physical well-being by recognizing what causes stress, using coping strategies, creating an affirming environment at home, and knowing when professional help is needed. This way, your retirement years can be as fulfilling and joyful as you've hoped.

1.7 ALTERNATIVE MEDICINE AND HOLISTIC APPROACHES IN RETIREMENT

As we delve into ways to maintain and improve our well-being in retirement, it becomes evident that traditional medicine is one piece of the puzzle. Many retirees use healing practices and holistic approaches to complement their healthcare regimens. These techniques often focus on alleviating symptoms and fostering wellness, which can be especially appealing as we strive to fully embrace our later years.

Explore Alternative Healthcare Options

Acupuncture, chiropractic care, and herbal medicine are a few alternative therapies that have gained popularity among the senior community. Each of these practices offers unique benefits. For instance, acupuncture, with its origins in ancient Chinese medicine, involves the insertion of thin needles into specific body points. It is widely used for pain relief and is believed to rebalance the energy flows within the body, which can lead to improved health outcomes. Chiropractic care focuses on disorders of the musculoskeletal and nervous systems and the effects these disorders have on general health. Many find that regular adjustments by a chiropractor help with pain management, increased mobility, and better alignment. Herbal medicine uses plants or mixtures of plant extracts to treat or prevent disease. It offers a natural approach that many find beneficial for maintaining health without the side effects sometimes associated with prescription drugs.

However, while the benefits can be significant, it's crucial to approach alternative medicine with caution. Not all practices are supported by robust scientific evidence, and the quality of practitioners can vary widely. Conduct thorough research and consult healthcare professionals before beginning any new treatment. Additionally, ensure that alternative therapies do not interfere with traditional medications or treatments, as interactions can sometimes lead to adverse effects.

> Quick Tip: In his book Lifeforce[12], Tony Robbins discusses the emerging area of regenerative medicine using stem cells. Explore this area for more information on pain management.

Integrating Holistic Health Practices

Incorporating health practices like yoga, Tai Chi, and aromatherapy into your routine can bring about many benefits. For example, yoga enhances balance while promoting well-being through meditation. It can be tailored to skill levels and primarily benefits those with limited mobility. Tai Chi, often described as moving meditation, is a form of exercise that reduces stress, improves balance, and boosts mood. Aromatherapy uses oils to

---

12. Robbins, A., Diamandis, P. H., & Hariri, R. (2022). *Life force: How new break-throughs in precision medicine can transform the quality of your life & those you love* (First Simon & Schuster hardcover edition). New York, NY: Simon & Schuster.

enhance physical and emotional well-being by benefiting the body, mind, and spirit.

> *Quick Tip: I first started practicing Tai Chi as a freshman in college, following four years of Tae Kwon Do in high school. I find Tai Chi relaxing, meditative, and helpful with my balance, flexibility, and overall aches and pains.*

You can join a local yoga class or follow instructional videos at home to incorporate these practices into your routine. Add Tai Chi sessions each week to maintain flexibility and balance. Using oils such as lavender or peppermint regularly can aid in stress management and enhance sleep quality. These activities contribute to well-being and promote relaxation.

Assessing the Effectiveness and Safety of Alternative Therapies

Start by researching sources that offer evidence supporting the treatments you are interested in. Consult healthcare professionals for advice regarding potential interactions with medications or health conditions. Consult certified practitioners from reputable organizations to ensure your selected therapies are safe and beneficial.

Case Studies and Personal Stories

Real-life examples can provide valuable insights into how alternative and holistic practices can effectively integrate into a retiree's healthcare regimen. For instance, consider the case of a retired nurse who found that regular chiropractic care helped her manage her chronic back pain better than medication alone. Or the veteran who discovered that tai chi classes improved his physical balance and helped him find mental peace, significantly reducing his stress levels. These stories can serve as powerful examples of the benefits of combining traditional and alternative treatments.

In summary, alternative medicine and holistic approaches offer valuable options for enhancing health and well-being in retirement. You can enjoy a more balanced and fulfilling lifestyle by carefully selecting and integrating these practices into your healthcare routine. Remember, the goal is to complement, not replace, traditional medical advice and treatments. As always, making informed decisions based on thorough research and professional advice will guide you toward the best outcomes for your health and happiness.

1.8 NAVIGATING MEDICARE, SUPPLEMENTAL, AND LONG-TERM INSURANCE

Unraveling the complexities of Medicare and different insurance choices may initially seem overwhelming, especially with 73% of people concerned that Medicare won't be there for them, according to a 2024 Survey on Aging in America.[13] However, with the proper understanding, you can make informed decisions that support your health and financial stability in retirement. Let's simplify the details of Medicare, compare insurance options, and explore the specifics of long-term care coverage so that you can select suitable plans for your situation.

Medicare is a health insurance program in the United States designed primarily for individuals aged 65 and above. It consists of 'parts' that address healthcare needs. Part A, known as hospital

---

13. Kiplinger Retirement Report. (2024, August). *Future US LLC*, New York, NY.

insurance, covers expenses related to inpatient hospital stays care in nursing facilities, hospice care, and some home health services. Most individuals do not have to pay a premium for Part A if they or their spouse contributed to Medicare taxes over the years. Part B provides insurance for doctor visits, outpatient services, medical supplies, and preventive care. It requires a monthly premium payment from beneficiaries. Part C, also known as Medicare Advantage, is an added option to Parts A and B. Offered by private companies approved by Medicare, it often includes extra benefits such as prescription drug coverage and dental or vision care. Finally, Part D, offered by the government, also provides coverage for prescription drugs, helping with the expenses of medications. It can be obtained through insurance companies. To check if a specific healthcare provider accepts Medicare, you can visit Medicare.gov/care-compare for help.

Enroll in Medicare at the proper time to avoid penalties and gaps in coverage. Your seven-month initial enrollment period begins three months before your 65th birthday month and ends three months after. Signing up on schedule ensures you steer clear of penalties and smoothly transition into this phase of life.

Deciding between Medigap (Medicare Supplement Insurance) and Medicare Advantage plans can significantly impact your healthcare journey. Medigap policies, sold by companies, help cover some healthcare costs that Original Medicare doesn't include, such as copayments, coinsurance, and deductibles. One key advantage of Medigap policies is the freedom to choose any provider who accepts Medicare; this flexibility is especially beneficial if you travel frequently or reside in different states during the year. However, Medigap typically does not include prescription drug coverage; for this, a separate Part D plan would be necessary.

Quick Tip: My parents had supplemental Medicare coverage for years, and before my mother passed away in 2022, she had several stays in the hospital, one of which was less than a week but totaled $25,000. Their bill and co-pay were zero because their supplemental Medicare policy covered everything.

On the other hand, Medicare Advantage plans might offer lower out-of-pocket costs and include additional benefits like dental, hearing, and vision care, which are not covered under Original Medicare. However, these plans usually have network restrictions, meaning you may have to see only doctors and facilities in the plan's network. Deciding between Medigap and Medicare Advantage often depends on your health needs, financial situation, and preference for flexibility versus comprehensive coverage. A Certified Financial Planner ® Professional can help walk you through the choices in more detail before you make an informed decision.

Prescription coverage under Medicare Part D is also vital, especially if you regularly take medications. Each Part D plan has a formulary and a list of covered drugs. Choosing a plan that best matches your medication needs can significantly reduce out-of-pocket costs. Reviewing your Part D coverage annually is advisable, as formularies can change, and what was once the best plan for your needs may no longer be. Recent changes in laws at the federal level will lower prescription costs through Medicare to only $35 for insulin, for example. Monitor your medications as more government cost-reduction negotiations are planned and authorized.

Reducing out-of-pocket expenses goes beyond choosing Medicare plans; it also involves reviewing your healthcare needs and coverage. Your health condition, medications, and financial situation can impact which plans suit you. During the Medicare Open Enrollment Period from October 15 to December 7, you can adjust your plans according to your requirements, potentially saving money and reducing stress.

Understanding long-term care insurance is important, since Medicare typically doesn't cover the long-term care that many people eventually need. Long-term care insurance can help cover financially burdensome services like in-home care, nursing home care, or assisted living facilities not included in Medicare. It is a proactive step in protecting your assets and ensuring quality care later in life.

Navigating through the complexities of Medicare and long-term care insurance ensures you have health coverage and safeguards your well-being, allowing you to enjoy retirement without unnecessary concerns. With details and thoughtful preparation, you can decide on options matching your healthcare requirements and retirement goals, bringing peace of mind to your family and yourself.

1.9 CREATING A HEALTH CARE PROXY AND ADVANCED MEDICAL DIRECTIVES

Deciding on directives and appointing a healthcare proxy are among our most significant choices when planning for the future. These decisions ensure that our medical care reflects our preferences when we cannot express them ourselves. Advanced medical directives outline what steps should be taken concerning our health if we cannot make those decisions due to illness or incapacity. This might involve directions on issues like whether to undergo life support in cases of disability or terminal illness.

These directives act as a guiding voice during times of crisis, helping loved ones and medical professionals to make decisions on your behalf.

Choosing a health care proxy, or durable power of attorney for health care, is equally crucial. This is a person you designate to make medical decisions on your behalf if you're incapacitated. The choice of who this person should be is significant and should not be taken lightly. It should be someone you trust implicitly, someone who understands your values and desires regarding medical treatments. Often, this might be a family member or a close friend. The key here is trust and their ability to handle stress, communicate effectively with medical personnel, and advocate fiercely for your wishes.

The legal formalization of these documents varies from state to state, and it's crucial to ensure they are set up correctly to be legally binding. Typically, this process involves filling out specific forms—either drafted by an attorney or obtained through reputable sources—and having them witnessed and notarized. Some states may have particular requirements about who must sign these forms, so it's essential to consult with a legal expert in your area or use state-provided resources to ensure everything is done correctly.

Discussing your medical wishes and the contents of your advanced directives with your family and doctors is not easy, but it is necessary. It ensures that everyone understands your preferences, which can prevent potential conflicts or confusion in critical moments. Start these discussions by being open about your values and what 'quality of life' means to you. Explain why you've made certain decisions in your directives, and listen to any concerns your loved ones might have. These conversations can be emotional, but they are also an opportunity to convey your wishes clearly and provide reassurance that these decisions align with how you want to be treated.

In handling these aspects of healthcare planning, we take control of our medical futures and provide clarity and guidance for our loved ones. This proactive approach allows us to communicate our wishes, ensuring that our healthcare aligns with our values and desires, even when we cannot express them ourselves. It's a profound gift to our families, removing the burden of making those tough decisions during a highly emotional time.

1.10 TECHNOLOGY: USING APPS AND DEVICES FOR HEALTH MANAGEMENT

In today's tech-driven world, the fusion of technology with health management for retirees is advantageous and genuinely transformative. As a retiree, using apps and devices dramatically improves your ability to oversee and maintain your health. This offers a level of immediacy and convenience that was once unimaginable. From apps that prompt you to take your medication to devices that monitor your heart rate and track your sleep patterns, technology provides tools that encourage an approach to looking after your health during retirement, putting you in control and fostering independence.

> *Quick Tip: Our sleep number bed tracks movements and assigns a sleep score based on restful versus restless sleep. This information has helped us adjust bad habits like watching TV in bed or leaving the lights on.*

Health management apps have proven invaluable for handling health routines. For instance, medication reminder apps play a role in managing medications by sending timely reminders to take your pills. This simple feature can make all the difference in adhering to your treatment regimen without relying on memory. Similarly, fitness-tracking apps offer a range of features, from tracking activities to providing motivational health advice. These apps also often include components for monitoring intake, helping you track what you eat, and facilitating a diet tailored to your health goals. By incorporating these apps into your schedule, you are fostering an approach to managing your health and empowering yourself with information and resources at your fingertips.

The rise of technology, such as fitness trackers and smartwatches, has transformed how we keep tabs on our well-being. These gadgets continually monitor health metrics like heart rate, activity levels, and even sleep patterns, offering a treasure trove of information to personalize health and fitness routines. For example, analyzing your heart rate trends during workouts can help you tailor your exercise regimen for fitness without pushing yourself too hard. Sleep tracking functions can also reveal insights into your sleep quality, prompting adjustments to bedtime habits for a night's sleep. The instant feedback from these wearables encourages informed decisions regarding your health habits, promoting a more adaptable and responsive approach to health management.

> *Quick Tip: My fitness band motivates me to reach 10,000 daily steps. If I am only at 7,000 steps, I realize I must get up and move to hit 10,000 steps. In the Army, we called them LPCs or Leather Personnel Carriers. These are your boots or shoes and are meant to carry you anywhere you need or want to go.*

Telemedicine has become an excellent option for retirees, especially those with mobility challenges or those living in remote areas. This technology allows you to consult with healthcare providers via video calls, reducing the need for physical travel. The convenience of receiving medical consultations from home not only saves time but also reduces the stress associated with frequent visits to the doctor's office. Telemedicine is advantageous for routine check-ups, follow-up visits, and minor medical queries that don't require physical exams. Moreover, it extends the reach of medical care, ensuring you have access to specialists' advice regardless of your location. This is crucial for those in less populated areas with limited medical resources.

While the benefits of integrating technology into health management are significant, we must be aware of concerns regarding data privacy and security. The personal nature of health data requires stringent measures to protect it from unauthorized access. When using health apps and devices, ensure that they comply with privacy laws and standards like the Health Insurance Portability and Accountability Act (HIPAA) in the United States. Be proactive in understanding the privacy policies of your apps and devices; ensure that your data is encrypted and you have control over how your information is shared. Regularly updating your devices and apps ensures the latest security measures protect you.

Furthermore, using strong passwords for your applications and enabling two-factor authentication will enhance data security. Exercise caution when sharing your health information. By following these steps, you can reap the benefits of using technology to manage your health without worrying much about the safety of your information.

Incorporating technology into your health routines can significantly improve how you take care of yourself. Whether through user apps that streamline health tasks, wearable devices that offer real-time health updates, or telemedicine services for convenient medical advice, technology empowers you to play an active and well-informed role in looking after your health. By being cautious and vigilant, you can use these tech tools to boost your well-being and ensure that your later years are more extended, healthier, and more satisfying.

STRATEGY 2 -
FINDING PURPOSE
LIVING YOUR PASSION

"If you don't know where you are going, any road will get you there." [1]

LEWIS CARROLL

D o you know where you are going? As the sun sets earlier each day and the chapters of our lives become quieter, many ponder a profound question: "What now?" You can only travel so much. If you're traveling one week each month, or 12 weeks in total, and that's a lot of travel, you must fill the other 40 weeks with something. Retirement, while a significant milestone, often brings a search for renewed meaning and purpose. It's common to feel a sense of 'drift' as the structured routines of our working years fade into memory. Yet, within this seemingly vast emptiness, a beautiful opportunity awaits—a chance to rediscover and reinvent oneself, to ignite passions that flickered in the back-

1.   Carroll, L. (n.d.). BrainyQuote. Retrieved from https://www.brainyquote.com/quotes/lewis_carroll_165865 , accessed on 8/20/24.

ground. At the same time, careers and raising families took center stage. In the exploration of purpose lies the key to transforming these years into some of the most fulfilling of your life. Being specific about your plan, what you want, and how to achieve it helps you say no to things that derail progress, distract your attention, and pull you off course.[2]

2.1 THE JAPANESE PHILOSOPHY OF DISCOVERING MEANING AND PURPOSE

The Japanese concept of Ikigai, which translates roughly to 'a reason for living,' beautifully encapsulates the pursuit of purpose. It's a compass that guides individuals toward a life that is not only meaningful but also joyful and fulfilling. Ikigai is often visualized at the intersection of four fundamental questions: What do you love? What are you good at? What does the world need from you? What can you be paid for? This framework doesn't just apply to professional endeavors; it encompasses all facets of life, encouraging a balance that fosters well-being and satisfaction. Life is not a problem to be solved. Just remember to have something that keeps you busy doing what you love while being surrounded by the people who love you.[3]

---

2. Clear, J. (2018). *Atomic habits: An easy and proven way to build good habits & break bad habits*. New York, NY: Penguin Random House.

3. García, H., Miralles, F., & Cleary, H. (2017). *Ikigai: The Japanese secret to a long and happy life*. Chicago / Turabian.

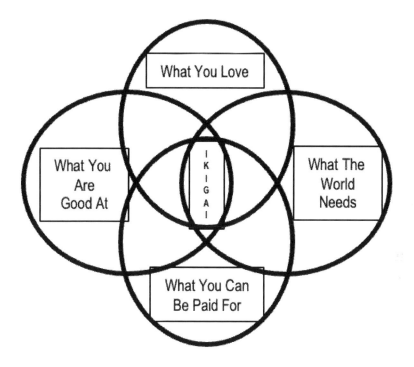

Figure 3. Ikigai Diagram

Purpose as Context

The pursuit of finding *purpose* is a theme that unites people worldwide. Different cultures emphasize the significance of discovering one's calling, a quest that adds richness and meaning to life. Whether it's the pursuit of the American Dream, which often centers on success and fulfillment, or the Bhutan Gross National Happiness Index, which evaluates prosperity based on the physical and environmental well-being of its citizens, the idea of purpose addresses a fundamental human need for connection, accomplishment, and happiness.

Understanding Ikigai

At its essence, Ikigai is about finding fulfillment. It prompts us to reflect on what keeps us engaged, brings us happiness, challenges us, and motivates us to start each day with enthusiasm. For some individuals, it may be gardening—a passion for nurturing growth and savoring the delights of nature. For others, it could involve mentoring and sharing insights gathered over a lifetime. Ikigai is a universal concept that provides a framework to help us align our actions with our innermost desires and contributions to society.

Components of Ikigai

The four components of Ikigai challenge us to integrate what we love (passion), what we are good at (vocation), what we can be paid for (profession), and what the world needs (mission). This holistic approach ensures that our pursuits are gratifying and valuable to others, creating a sense of accomplishment and contribution. For example, a retired teacher might find that tutoring disadvantaged students aligns with her skills and passions and meets an acute need in the community, providing her income and a profound sense of purpose.

Implementing Ikigai

Incorporating Ikigai into your life begins with self-reflection. Use the space provided in Exercise 1 below to start by outlining responses to the four questions of Ikigai. Reflect on activities that captivate you, tasks that don't feel like work areas where you can make an impact, and how you can translate these insights into a fulfilling retirement strategy. For example, if you have always had a passion for history and possess research skills, consider volun-

teering at a museum or launching a blog that shares your knowledge with the community.

Exercise 1. Finding Your Ikigai

What do you love to do?

_____

_____

_____

What are you good at?

_____

_____

_____

What does the world need?

_____

_____

_____

What can you be paid for?

_____

_____

_____

Look at the overlap and intersection of the four areas from Figure
3. It's in this space that your unique ikigai resides. Spend some
time trying to identify the area of overlap that particularly

resonates with you and that you can articulate clearly. Please write it down and review it with friends and your significant other for feedback. Every step to align your actions with your Ikigai brings you closer to a life defined not by what you leave in retirement but by what you have the potential to gain. Incorporating the essence of Ikigai into your retirement plans unlocks opportunities for happiness, satisfaction, and involvement. It involves striking a balance among your passions, skills, societal needs you can address, and avenues that offer emotional benefits. This journey towards uncovering your Ikigai is more than about passing the time —it's about enriching your existence with meaning and enthusiasm, making each day purposeful and deliberate.

> *Quick Tip: Famed architect Frank Lloyd Wright, perhaps the first genuine knowledge worker, discovered his ikigai at age 20. He continued to create architectural masterpieces, culminating in the Guggenheim Art Museum in New York City, on which he continued working until he passed away at age 91.*

2.2 REDISCOVERING YOUR IDENTITY AFTER RETIREMENT

Retirement unfolds a canvas that many find unexpectedly blank. After decades of painting your days with the familiar strokes of work routines and family responsibilities, this new freedom, though liberating, can sometimes feel overwhelming. Where does one start when faced with the opportunity to finally focus on desires that may have been set aside for career and family? This chapter gently guides you through rediscovering those muted passions and interests, helping you sketch a vibrant, fulfilling picture of your retirement life. According to the book *Finding*

Flow[4], 'What we do day in and day out has a lot to do with what kind of life we have; how we experience what we do is even more important.'

Exploring Your Interests

Begin by delving into your present interests—a sort of archaeological exploration into your past experiences and dreams that may have been put on hold. Find a tranquil space for this introspection, a corner where you can reflect without distractions. Equip yourself with a journal and jot down activities that used to bring you joy, projects that piqued your curiosity but remained unexplored, or skills you always wanted to develop but never had the chance to do so. This exercise goes beyond recollection; it's about reconnecting with facets of yourself that might have been overlooked over time.

Embrace these interests without judgment, whether painting, writing poetry, playing an instrument, tournament fishing, or tending to a garden. Reflect on the emerging themes. Are you inclined towards expression, outdoor pursuits, problem-solving, or fostering innovation?

> *Quick Tip: In his book UNRETIRED, Mark S. Walton quotes an interviewee as saying, "We may lose our bodily strength as we get older, but we don't lose our creativity until the minister or doctor closes our eyes."* [5] *I found this valid with former Secretary of State and Nobel Peace Prize winner Dr. Henry Kissinger, whom I met in 2016 when he*

---

4. Csikszentmihalyi, M. (1997). *Finding flow: The psychology of engagement with everyday life*. New York, NY: Basic Books.
5. Walton, M. S. (2024). *Unretired: How highly effective people live happily ever after*. New York, NY: Profit Research Inc.

*was 92. Despite being in a wheelchair and unable to stand
or walk, he was sharp as a tack, answering questions from a
friendly and curious panel of Army General officers.*

Setting New Goals

With your rediscovered interests laid bare, the next step is to align
them with realistic, achievable goals. This alignment is crucial; it
ensures that your pursuits are not just whims but sustainable
passions that enrich your life in retirement. For example, if you've
uncovered a love for painting, plan to enroll in a painting course at
a local community center or online. If travel and culture were
always your passions, plan to visit a new country each year or
explore the diverse cultural offerings closer to home. Make these
goals specific and time-bound, giving yourself the clarity and dead-
line that turn intentions into actions. Remember, the aim here is
not to fill every hour of your day but to enrich your days with
purpose and pleasure.

> *Quick Tip: We use SMART goals to achieve more in the
> military: goals that are Specific, Measurable, Achievable,
> Relevant, and Timebound.*

Case Studies of Reinvention

Consider the story of Maria, a former bank executive whose
passion for photography was reignited in her retirement. She
transformed this passion into a thriving community project,
capturing the stories of her city's most historic neighborhoods and
their residents. Her exhibitions, initially online and later in local
community centers, fulfilled her creative spirit and reconnected
her with her community, giving her a new sense of belonging and

purpose. Then there's James, a retired teacher who turned his love for woodworking into a small business, crafting custom furniture. His venture supplemented his income and connected him with young artisans with whom he shares his skills, fulfilling a passion for teaching in a new realm.

Exploring Resources

Numerous resources are available to help you explore and expand your rekindled interests. Local libraries and community centers offer a wealth of information, providing classes ranging from art to technology. Organizations like the Osher Lifelong Learning Institutes (OLLI) provide courses to retirees, promoting learning within a supportive community setting. Websites such as Meetup.com connect individuals with local interests, whether hiking, reading, or photography. Engage with these resources as they serve as pathways to acquiring skills and forming connections with like-minded individuals who share your enthusiasm.

Discovering Artistic Talents

If your reflections indicate a love for expression, now is the moment to develop or uncover your artistic talents. Art in all its forms offers therapeutic advantages by improving mental well-being and emotional health. Start with beginner classes that allow you to learn without the pressure of perfection. Try art media like watercolors, acrylics, digital art, or pottery. Each has appeal and challenges, offering new ways to express your thoughts and feelings. Remember, the focus should be on enjoying the process and gaining enrichment rather than striving for flawless results.

Quick Tip: My father discovered a knack for painting in his 30s and completed about a half dozen large-format paintings. One of his paintings hangs in our home. During a recent trip, he discussed his desire to start painting again - at age 85.

By rediscovering these aspects of yourself, you are not just passing the time—you are infusing your life with meaning and happiness. Each step you take, each choice you make, and each new exploration is like a brushstroke on the canvas of your retirement years, turning it into a masterpiece of satisfaction and ongoing growth.

2.3 VOLUNTEERING: GIVING BACK AND GAINING MORE

Every thread of experience you've woven carries its unique hue and strength in the tapestry of life. Retirement unveils the time and opportunity to contribute these vibrant threads to the societal fabric through volunteering. This endeavor is not just about filling time; it's a profound journey into recapturing your sense of purpose, giving back to the community, and rediscovering personal joy and fulfillment. As you consider the vast landscape of volunteering, start by aligning your efforts with causes that resonate deeply with your values and passions. Whether nurturing abandoned pets, mentoring young students, or planting community gardens, your chosen activity should mirror your deepest convictions and interests.

Identify Causes of Personal Significance

Start by reflecting on what moves you. What societal challenges pull at your heartstrings, or what past experiences have shaped your understanding of need in the world? It could be anything from education, environmental conservation, health care, and veterans to social justice. Allow your life's journey and professional expertise to guide your choice. A former educator might find immense joy in tutoring underserved children, directly influencing their futures. Meanwhile, someone passionate about environmental conservation might thrive in volunteer work related to wildlife conservation or public park maintenance. The key here is to connect your journey and passions with the world's needs, creating a fulfilling alignment that nourishes you and those you help.

Benefits of Volunteering

The benefits of volunteering stretch far beyond the simple act of giving. Studies have shown that volunteering can significantly enhance mental and physical health. A report from the Corporation for National and Community Service highlights a strong relationship between volunteering and health: those who volunteer have lower mortality rates, more extraordinary functional ability, and lower rates of depression later in life than those who do not. The social aspect of volunteering also cannot be overstated; it connects you with others, helping to build a supportive community network. These social interactions can be particularly beneficial, warding off loneliness and depression, common challenges in later life. The activity involved in specific volunteer work can also improve your physical health, keeping you active and agile.

> *Quick Tip: For the last ten years, labyrinth artist Denny Dyke has been creating paths called Circles in the Sand that attract thousands each Summer to the beaches of western Oregon. There is no cost for anyone to enjoy the 2-*

hour walk in the maze along the coast; donations are
accepted at sandypathbandon.com. Imagine the joy Denny
and his volunteer helpers have given so many people.

Finding Volunteer Opportunities

Finding one that matches your interests and physical capabilities is essential when looking for volunteer opportunities. Start by visiting community centers, libraries, or non-profit organizations to ask about their volunteer needs. Websites like VolunteerMatch.org and Idealist.org can also help you find opportunities that suit your skills and passions based on location. Remember to talk to friends who volunteer; they can give you advice and might even join you in this experience.

> *Quick Tip: Try any associations you might be affiliated*
> *with first. My affiliation with the Financial Planning*
> *Association led to volunteer opportunities with Homes For*
> *Our Troops and the Coordinated Assistance Network. Both*
> *are centered on helping veterans, a particular passion of*
> *mine.*

Case Studies of Successful Retiree Volunteers

Take, for example, Linda, a retired nurse who found a renewed sense of purpose by volunteering at a local free clinic. Utilizing her lifelong skills, she not only aids those in need of medical care but also mentors younger volunteers aspiring to enter the healthcare field. Her presence is a bridge between generations, sharing invaluable knowledge and compassion. Then there's Michael, a retired engineer, who volunteers with an organization that builds homes for needy families. His expertise ensures the structural integrity of these homes and brings him immense satisfaction in knowing his work has a lasting impact on the community.

Volunteering during retirement allows you to embark on a journey where your life experiences can keep growing and inspiring others. It provides satisfaction and societal benefits, enhancing your life and those around you. Taking on this role means bringing the wisdom gained over the years and the drive to create change, showing that retirement isn't the end of a career but a continuation of contributing to an existence.

2.4 LIFELONG LEARNING: CLASSES, WORKSHOPS, AND ONLINE EDUCATION

Pursuing knowledge and personal development continues even after retirement but thrives without the constraints of a full-time job. Embracing learning during retirement can lead to cognitive and social benefits that enhance your overall quality of life. Engaging in pursuits not only keeps the brain active but also has the potential to delay age-related cognitive decline. Moreover, learning in a group setting, whether physically or mentally, promotes interactions that are crucial for mental and emotional well-being, helping to combat feelings of isolation often experienced during retirement.

Benefits of Continuous Learning

Learning itself can be incredibly refreshing as it challenges the mind and nurtures critical thinking and problem-solving abilities, keeping the brain sharp. Each new skill acquired serves as a boost against the effects of aging. Furthermore, participating in classroom discussions or group projects, whether online or offline, provides opportunities for engagement that foster a sense of community and belonging, ultimately enhancing wellness and a feeling of connectedness. The joy of learning new subjects or mastering new skills also boosts self-esteem and contributes to a more positive outlook on life—an excellent antidote to the 'blues' that sometimes shadow retirement.

Options for Learning

For those eager to dive into learning, options are plentiful. Local community colleges often offer a range of courses designed specifically for retirees, providing skill development and a vibrant community of peers. For a more flexible schedule, online platforms like Coursera or Udemy offer courses on almost any topic imaginable, from the intricacies of ancient history to the basics of computer programming. These platforms allow you to learn at your own pace, from the comfort of your home, often for free or at a minimal cost. Additionally, universities usually have extension programs or institutes for continuing education that provide more structured learning experiences, sometimes even with the opportunity to earn certificates or degrees.

> *Quick Tip: Check out language apps to start learning a new language. Tie this new goal to a habit such as breakfast. Every day at breakfast, begin with 5 minutes of practice and then, in subsequent months, increase by five more minutes to 10 minutes, etc. Before long, you'll be conversational in another language.*

Engaging with Learning Communities

Joining study groups or online forums can significantly enhance the learning experience. These communities provide support, broaden perspectives, and deepen understanding through discussion and collaboration. They can be precious when tackling more challenging subjects, where a group's collective knowledge and encouragement can propel you forward. Local libraries or learning centers often host such groups, and many online courses also offer forums where students worldwide can connect, discuss, and support each other's learning journeys.

Leveraging Free and Low-Cost Resources

Beyond the structured environments of courses and workshops, a wealth of free or low-cost educational resources are available for those searching for knowledge. Libraries are invaluable, offering books, magazines, DVDs, and access to online resources and lectures. Many museums offer free entry days or discounted rates for seniors, and they often hold lectures and workshops that allow more profound engagement with their exhibits. Additionally, websites like Khan Academy provide free courses on various subjects at all levels, making learning accessible to everyone. These resources make it possible to explore new territories of knowledge without committing to more formal class settings or hefty tuition fees.

> *Quick Tip: Check out TED talks online and YouTube for great videos on learning new household upkeep tasks, such as fixing a toilet, repairing a lawn sprinkler system, or wallpapering a bedroom.*

By embracing learning, you are not merely passing the time—you are ensuring that your retirement years are filled with enrichment and vibrancy. You are stimulating your intellect, broadening your horizons, and forming connections with others. The quest for knowledge enriches your life and serves as a model for future generations, showing that personal growth and progress continue throughout one's lifetime, even after retirement. It provides a sense of purpose, keeping you motivated and engaged.

2.5 MENTORSHIP ROLES: SHARING YOUR KNOWLEDGE AND EXPERIENCE

Mentorship associated with business settings or bustling university environments takes on a unique and profoundly satisfying role in retirement. Picture using your life experiences to guide and inspire someone at the start of their journey. This mutual exchange goes beyond sharing knowledge; it rejuvenates your purpose and forges connections between generations, building bridges that enrich both sides. The beauty of mentorship lies in the shared growth it nurtures—mentees gain insights and support, while mentors find renewed joy in witnessing their legacies carried forward by others.

Advantages of Being a Mentor

Being a mentor can bring great fulfillment. It's a way to pass on your earned wisdom and expertise, but more importantly, it brings emotional satisfaction from watching someone thrive under your guidance. This can be especially meaningful in retirement, where thoughts about professional legacies often take the stage. Engaging with individuals can also help keep you alert and socially connected, offsetting feelings of isolation. Furthermore, mentees' enthusiasm and fresh viewpoints can be refreshing, often sparking ideas or passions and nurturing a sense of continuous personal growth.

Exploring Mentorship Opportunities

Discovering suitable avenues for mentorship might seem overwhelming at first. Some resources facilitate these valuable connections. Organizations such as SCORE, backed by the U.S. Small Business Administration, provide platforms for retired professionals to mentor aspiring entrepreneurs. Here, your business knowledge and expertise can directly contribute to the development of businesses, offering a meaningful channel for your talents. Educational institutions frequently look for volunteers to guide and assist students in their fields of study, whether through tutoring, career guidance, or life skills coaching. Online platforms dedicated to mentorship, like MentorCruise, also offer opportunities to connect with mentees globally, enabling engagement that suits your retirement lifestyle.

Best Practices in Mentorship

Successful mentorship hinges on establishing a supportive relationship. It involves listening, empathy, and motivation to nurture the mentee's development and self-assurance. Begin each mentoring connection by outlining expectations and objectives. What does the mentee aim to accomplish? How can you offer support? Regular face-to-face or virtual meetings help keep the relationship moving and ensure a constant flow of feedback. It's vital to foster communication and honesty, allowing mentees to discuss triumphs and challenges openly. The ultimate aim is to provide guidance rather than impose directives. Encourage mentees to take charge of their decisions. Offer advice and a broader perspective on rules. This approach helps nurture their thinking skills and decision-making abilities, critical elements of professional growth.

> *Quick Tip: I mentored people in all three of my pre-retire-ment roles, and the best advice I can offer is to ask many questions, such as: Why do you think that is the best option? Have you considered other alternatives? These questions get people to think about their answers.*

Case Studies of Successful Mentor-Mentee Relationships

Consider the case of Robert, a retired engineer who mentored a young environmental scientist developing sustainable building materials. Through their sessions, Robert shared his extensive knowledge of materials engineering and insights on navigating the professional landscape. The mentee launched a startup based on sustainable materials, attributing much of his success to Robert's guidance and steadfast support. Then there's Sarah, a former school principal, who mentored new educators in her community, helping them to develop effective teaching strategies and manage classroom dynamics. Her mentees speak of the confidence and skills they gained, which they attribute directly to her mentoring. These stories highlight the transfer of knowledge and the profound personal connections and mutual benefits that are the heart of mentorship.

Getting involved in mentoring opens a chapter in your lifelong learning journey in which your accomplishments have an impact. Mentorship consists of passing on wisdom to illuminate someone's path, shining your light brightly, and maintaining meaningful connections with others. Through mentorship, retirement isn't a time for reflection—it's an opportunity to contribute actively, drawing on your wealth of experiences to bring value, happiness, and purpose to others.

2.6 STAYING SOCIAL: BUILDING AND MAINTAINING NEW FRIENDSHIPS

As we enter our retirement years, how we engage socially tends to shift. The vibrant workplace conversations are replaced by days that hold promise but may need more social interactions. I can't emphasize enough the importance of staying socially connected during this period because these relationships affect our emotional and physical well-being. Extensive research has highlighted the benefits of relationships in promoting longevity[6] and reducing the risk of various health issues like depression and high blood pressure. Building and nurturing old and new friendships isn't just an activity—it's a key aspect of leading a fulfilling retired life. We will explore this topic in even greater detail to build resilience in Chapter 4.

Importance of Social Connections

The significance of connections lies in how they bring joy into our lives and provide us with a sense of belonging and purpose. They are our link to the world, offering a platform to share our successes and struggles. Losing the daily interactions of the work environment underscores our need to cultivate and sustain relationships actively. These connections can offer support while encouraging

---

6.   Waldinger, R., & Schulz, M. (2023). *The good life*. New York, NY: Simon & Schuster.

and sharing joy in moments of triumph. Having friends around you is priceless. Their presence provides comfort and understanding that enriches your life with happiness and insight, which can be hard to achieve alone. 'According to scientists who have studied the five *Blue Zones*, the keys to longevity are diet, exercise, finding a purpose in life (an ikigai), and forming strong social ties-that is, having a broad circle of friends and good family relations.'[7]

> *Quick Tip: Next time you're on a plane, train, or bus next to someone or standing by someone in line, introduce yourself and ask them about their unique story. Everyone has a story; if only you would ask. You may end up making a new friend for life.*

Making New Connections

One way to expand your circle is by joining clubs or groups that cater to your interests. Whether it's a gardening club, a book club, a sports league like pickleball, or even a local country club, these organizations offer structured opportunities for meeting like-minded individuals. Attending community events is another way to engage with people in your neighborhood. Festivals, art exhibitions, and lectures can be more enjoyable when shared. Additionally, online platforms such as Facebook or Meetup can be tools for connecting with groups and events. These platforms often feature groups focused on photography, hiking, or cooking, making finding and bonding with people with similar interests more straightforward.

---

7. García, H., Miralles, F., & Cleary, H. (2017). *Ikigai: The Japanese secret to a long and happy life.* Chicago / Turabian.

Nurturing Relationships

Keeping up with friendships takes effort and dedication, especially as life circumstances evolve. Stay in touch through calls, messages, emails, or social media to nurture these bonds. Planning hangouts, like coffee meetups, lunches, movie nights, or even trips together, can help create shared memories and strengthen relationships. Being there for each other during challenging times by offering support and a listening ear can deepen friendships and establish a foundation of trust and mutual care.

> *Quick Tip: I use Facebook to stay updated with friends and catch up in person when we meet for lunch or a happy hour event. We then don't have to hash out everything that's transpired in the last few months, but we can hit the highlights since I've been following them and can start talking about how they are doing now in real-time.*

Dealing With Social Anxiety

Meeting individuals and attending social gatherings can be challenging for people who have been away from such situations for a time. Feeling anxious in these settings is quite common. Some strategies can be used to cope with these feelings effectively. Start small, with a coffee chat, with a neighbor, or by joining a small book club gathering. Slowly expand your circle, allowing yourself to feel more at ease as time passes. Being prepared can help reduce anxiety; having some conversation topics ready can boost your confidence in social settings. Consider taking a communication skills class or attending a workshop on building trust. These avenues offer tips and the chance to connect with others with similar struggles.

Quick Tip: Make the interaction about the other person and not you. Act as a reporter and ask many questions, then listen intently and ask follow-up questions. I guarantee they will think you are warm, friendly, and brilliant.

By weaving these connections into the fabric of your retired life, you ensure that your days are enriched with activities and relationships that bring happiness, support, and a sense of belonging. These social ties can transform the canvas of your retirement years into a masterpiece filled with laughter, shared tales, and mutual encouragement.

2.7 PART-TIME WORK AND EXTRA INCOME AFTER RETIREMENT

After retiring, many envision a life of relaxation and freedom from the grind of a job. However, some discover that engaging in part-time work or finding ways to earn income can bring structure, fulfillment, and financial stability to their retirement years. Pursuing opportunities for part-time employment or exploring avenues for income can add purpose and variety to your routine. This could involve utilizing your expertise through consulting gigs or indulging in hobbies like photography or crafting that have the potential to generate revenue.

For those transitioning from full-time work to retirement, consulting in their field of expertise can be a way to stay engaged. Tutoring is also a choice for individuals with a background in education or specialized knowledge in math, science, or languages. If you have a talent for creating crafts, platforms like Etsy offer an outlet to sell your items. Additionally, photography enthusiasts can monetize their passion by selling photos on stock websites, providing photography services for events, or collaborating with businesses. House sitting in sought-after locations can be a way to explore new places and cultures.

The key to making the most of this opportunity is to figure out what you enjoy and what is practical for you, striking a balance between pleasure and potential earnings. This equilibrium ensures that your retirement pursuits bring satisfaction rather than stress, aligning perfectly with the goal of a fulfilling retirement.

Quick Tip: The bonus section at the back of this book contains the URL link to my 20 Extra Income Ideas, which can be downloaded for FREE.

How to Find Meaningful Part-Time Work

Securing part-time work that is personally fulfilling and financially lucrative requires planning, especially when transitioning from a full-time career to flexible retirement employment. Begin by updating your resume to showcase your work history and emphasize skills and experiences relevant to your current job search. Using a resume may benefit retirees since it allows you to highlight your skills and accomplishments without focusing on specific employment dates.

Networking continues to be a method of finding employment opportunities.

Utilize your connections to engage in local community organizations or hobby groups. Feel free to use social media platforms such as LinkedIn to establish connections with potential employers or clients. Networking often uncovers hidden opportunities and introduces you to individuals who appreciate the expertise and insights that come with experience.

Navigating job interviews as a retiree presents its set of challenges. Be prepared to discuss how your age brings value by offering reliability, experience, and a mature outlook on the position. Demonstrate your abilities and enthusiasm for the role to address any concerns employers may have regarding your tech proficiency or stamina. Emphasizing your eagerness to learn and adapt and your honed problem-solving skills can position you well as a candidate.

Adapting Skills to New Industries

Exploring part-time work options in retirement opens up chances to transition into industries that have always piqued your interest but still need to be explored. Start by evaluating your skills—leadership, project management, communication, and problem-solving are sought-after attributes. Consider how these skills can be applied across roles or sectors. Having a background in management could prove helpful in a role that involves overseeing volunteers and fundraising efforts. Also, the type of education or certification needed to transition into an industry should be considered. Many community colleges and online platforms offer short-term courses that can provide the knowledge and credentials to help bridge the gap between your experience and new opportunities. Pursuing these can be beneficial both intellectually and professionally, making you more attractive in a different field.

Legal and Financial Considerations

Although working part-time during retirement can have advantages, knowing the legal and financial consequences and how additional income might impact your social security benefits or pension is crucial. If you recently left work, please ensure you are not subject to a non-compete agreement or restricted concerning certain activities for some time. Check with your ethics office for details. For example, income from part-time work can affect your benefits, particularly if you still need to reach full retirement age (FRA). Ensure that the earnings limit is understood since exceeding it could reduce social security benefits if exceeded before FRA. See SSA.Gov for more info.

Moreover, the tax implications of earning income should be considered. Knowing how much you must pay in taxes and whether you need to make estimated tax payments can help you manage your finances effectively and avoid any surprises come tax season. Talking to a financial consultant who grasps the intricacies of retirement funds can be extremely helpful in making sure that your part-time job fits well with your long-term objectives and requirements.

Examining these factors allows you to make financial and personal choices to improve your retirement. This enables you to pursue work that brings fulfillment and a feeling of accomplishment without jeopardizing your stability or leisure time. Striking this balance is crucial for a fulfilling and pleasant retirement.

2.8 STARTING A SMALL BUSINESS OR SIDE HUSTLE AFTER 50

Colonel Harland Sanders, founder of Kentucky Fried Chicken, inspires those looking to embark on new business ventures later in life. At 65, when most would consider retiring, Sanders used his first social security check to fund a venture that would eventually become a global phenomenon. His story isn't just about creating a successful business; it's about redefining the possibilities of later life. Sanders faced numerous rejections before his unique blend of herbs and spices caught on, proving that perseverance and passion can lead to success at any age. His journey illustrates that the golden years can be a time of remarkable entrepreneurial activity and that pursuing your dreams has no expiration date.

Evaluating Business Ideas

The first step for those inspired to start a business post-retirement is evaluating your business ideas. Start with what you know and love. Your years of experience have likely endowed you with specialized knowledge and skills that can form the foundation of a successful business. Consider how these can meet a need in the market. Research is necessary here—understand who your customers might be, what they need, and how your skills can serve those needs. Also, consider the scalability of your ideas; while some businesses may require significant upfront investment, others can start small and expand over time. It's also prudent to assess the financial implications—how much money would you need to start, and what are the prospects for return on investment? This evaluation should align with your financial goals and how much you're willing to risk, ensuring your venture enhances your retirement rather than jeopardizing it.

Steps to Start a Small Business

Once you've honed your idea, the next step is laying the ground-work to turn it into reality. Begin by formalizing your business structure. Depending on your business, this could range from a sole proprietorship to an LLC or a corporation, each with its legal and tax implications. The next step is registering your business with local and state authorities and obtaining the necessary licenses and permits. Next, focus on how you'll finance your startup. While personal savings might be an immediate source, consider other options like small business loans, grants, or partnering with other entrepreneurs. Setting up a detailed business plan is crucial as it helps map out the specifics of your business operations and secure financing. Marketing your business effectively is also vital. In today's digital age, a well-designed website and active social media presence must be effective. Traditional marketing methods such as local advertising and word-of-mouth should not be overlooked, as they can be precious for community-focused businesses.

Mentorship and Networking

Navigating the complexities of a new business is challenging, making mentorship and networking invaluable. Engaging with local entrepreneur groups and business associations can provide support and guidance that is crucial in the early stages of your business. These groups offer a wealth of resources, from networking opportunities and partnerships to workshops and seminars that can help sharpen your business acumen. Finding a mentor who has gone through the entrepreneurial journey can provide you with insights and guidance that only experience can teach. A mentor can offer technical advice and moral support, helping you navigate setbacks and focus on your goals. Once again, The Service Core Of Retired Executives (SCORE) is an excellent resource for mentors and assistance.

Balancing a Business with a Retirement Lifestyle

Starting a business after 50 should also harmonize with the lifestyle you envision for retirement. It's important to set boundaries that allow you to enjoy retirement benefits while running your business. This might mean setting specific work hours, outsourcing certain tasks, or partnering with others to share the workload. Remember, your business's goal should be financial success and enhancing the quality of your life, allowing you to engage in meaningful and fulfilling activities.

> *Quick Tip: Please don't bite off more than you can chew. My parents started a small ice cream shop in their early 60s, and they soon found themselves overwhelmed with the long hours and various responsibilities involved in running and managing the business, from daily operations to cleaning and paperwork duties.*

By embracing entrepreneurship in retirement, you embark on a journey where your lifelong skills and interests can thrive, impacting those around you. Whether it entails transforming a hobby into an enterprise or applying your expertise in a fresh, adaptable setting, the possibilities are vast and limited only by your creativity. Through planning, a grasp of your objectives, and a dedication to striking a balance between work and leisure activities, you can ensure that this venture is successful and enriching as part of your 'post-fifty' life journey. As Peter Roesler notes in his book *How to Start a Business, the Quick and Easy Guide*, starting a business can be exciting and rewarding. "It's more than just chasing the dream of financial freedom or calling the shots as your own boss. It's about making a profound impact, imprinting a lasting legacy of your life and the lives of others. Plus, it's fun. You can change the world."[8]

2.9 BUILDING AND LEAVING A LEGACY

The concept of a legacy often conjures images of grand financial bequests or monumental institutions bearing one's name. Yet, the true essence of a legacy stretches far beyond the confines of material wealth. It encompasses the values you've upheld, the lessons you've imparted, and your impact on your community and family. A well-rounded legacy is an amalgamation of your life's work and passions, a lasting imprint that continues to influence and inspire even after you've stepped back.

Defining a Personal Legacy

Think of your legacy as your footprint on the world—a collection of marks reflecting your journey, beliefs, and actions. It's about how you've touched people's lives through kindness, leadership, creativity, or service. This legacy includes the wisdom you've shared, the love you've spread, and how you've lived your life according to your values. It's about the character you've built and the character you've helped build in others, the courage you've shown, and the courage you've inspired in your family and friends. Understanding this broadens the perspective of what it means to leave a legacy—it's not just what you do for people, but what you leave in people.

---

8.   Roesler, P., (2024) How to Start a Business, the Quick and Easy Guide, KDP

Steps for Planning Your Legacy

When planning your legacy, there are steps to consider, including practical, financial, and personal aspects—ensuring that your will and any trusts are kept current and clear and truly reflect your wishes. These legal documents play a role in ensuring that your financial legacy is distributed in line with your intentions. In addition, think about creating a personal testimonial – a more informal document to share your values, experiences, and life lessons. This can be a way to pass on the tangible parts of your legacy. Contact an attorney who specializes in these areas for additional information. You might also want to document your life story through written memoirs or video recordings. These personal reflections allow you to share your journey and offer insights and wisdom that can inspire generations.

Engaging in Philanthropy

Engaging in philanthropic activities is a noble and strategic way to build your legacy and promote your values into the future. Start by identifying causes that deeply resonate with what you believe in. Whether supporting education, advancing research or protecting the environment, your charitable contributions can significantly affect areas that matter most to you. Managing donations requires logistical support, but you could also think about setting up scholarships, endowments, or giving back through volunteering opportunities. You contribute to your legacy every time you give, incorporating your interests and beliefs into the community fabric.

2.10 TECHNOLOGY FOR CONNECTIVITY AND CONVENIENCE

In an evolving tech-driven world, embracing technology can revolutionize how you stay connected with others, manage your well-being, and enjoy entertainment. This digital shift can significantly enrich your life during retirement by providing ways to keep in touch with loved ones, monitor health effectively, and access a wide range of cultural and intellectual content from the comfort of your own home.

Embracing the World of Technology

Think of technology not as a wave to be feared for its force but as a current that can carry you to new experiences, deeper relationships, and greater well-being. The initial step is often the hardest—overcoming hesitations about its complexity or role in your life. Start with the basics: learn to use a smartphone or tablet to connect with family and friends via video calls, messaging apps, or social media. These tools have become lifelines for many, shrinking distances and bringing faces and voices into each other's homes, making conversations and shared moments possible despite physical separation.

> *Quick Tip: I wish I used FaceTime more often with my grandkids. I worked on a project 30 years ago to offer video phone services to grandparents as a monthly subscription. Today, you can do this for FREE on your mobile device. I hope you'll use it regularly to stay connected.*

Senior Friendly Tech Tools

Modern businesses are becoming more mindful of the requirements of more mature adults regarding technology, resulting in various easy-to-use tools tailored to improve accessibility and user experience. Regarding health monitoring, explore smartwatches that monitor heart rate and physical activity or apps that help you remember your medication schedule. You can also find versions of smartphones and tablets with icons, text, voice commands, and simple navigation features. Additionally, you can boost home security with gadgets like security cameras, motion sensors, and emergency response systems for added peace of mind for you and your loved ones.

Online Safety Tips

While the internet offers benefits, navigating it to safeguard yourself from scams and privacy breaches is essential. Keep your software up to date to shield against threats. Use unique passwords for each account. Consider using a password manager for secure storage. Exercise caution when dealing with emails or messages asking for information or directing you to unfamiliar websites—phishing scams are prevalent and increasingly sophisticated. It's also wise to review the privacy settings on your social media accounts to manage who can access your information and posts. By keeping yourself updated on risks and practicing careful behavior while using the internet, you can experience the advantages of technology with added security.

*Quick Tip: My 85-year-old dad was the victim of a
phishing scam by inadvertently clicking on a suspicious
link in an email. I highly recommend virus protection software for everyone. Please DO NOT click on emails or texts
without virus protection.*

Learning Platforms

There are resources for those interested in expanding their
knowledge of technology. Many community centers and libraries
conduct workshops for seniors, providing hands-on training.
Online platforms such as TechBoomers and Senior Planet offer
tutorials customized for individuals, covering topics ranging from
computer skills to more advanced lessons on using apps and social
media. These platforms simplify technology. They empower you
to utilize tools effectively, enhancing your independence and interaction with the world around you.

By incorporating technology into your routine, you unlock opportunities for connections, improved health management, and
broader exploration of cultural and intellectual offerings worldwide. It's about leveraging these tools to enhance your life without
overwhelming it, enabling you to embrace an increasingly interconnected world.

By using these insights and tools, you'll be well-equipped to navigate the world of technology confidently. It's about starting on the
right foot, confident that you have the know-how to make the most
of these tools to enrich your life and expand your horizons.

As we progress, remember that each aspect of technology we've
discussed helps enhance parts of your life and connects with
broader themes like staying engaged, informed, and secure during

your retirement years. It's not just about using technology; it's about integrating it into your routine in a way that brings value, happiness, and convenience every day. Let's continue this journey as we delve into aspects of a fulfilling retirement in the following chapters.

MAKE A DIFFERENCE WITH YOUR REVIEW
UNLOCK THE POWER OF GENEROSITY

"Money can't buy happiness, but giving it away can."

FREDDIE MERCURY

People who give without expecting anything in return live longer, happier lives and even make more money! So, during our time together, I want to try this idea.

I have a question for you...

Would you help someone you've never met, even if you never got credit for it?

Who is this person, you ask? They are like you—or, at least, like you used to be. They want to make a difference and need help, but they need help figuring out where to look.

My mission is to make retirement planning easy for everyone. Everything I do stems from that mission, and the only way to accomplish it is by reaching...well...everyone.

This is where you come in. Most people do judge a book by its cover (and its reviews). So here's my ask on behalf of a struggling adult you've never met:

Please help that adult by leaving this book a review.

Your gift costs no money and takes less than 60 seconds to make real, but it can change a fellow adult's life forever. Your review could help...

- One more person plan a happy retirement.
- One more family enjoy their time together.
- One more person find peace and purpose in their later years.

To get that 'feel good' feeling and help this person for real, all you have to do is...and it takes less than 60 seconds...leave a review.

Simply scan the QR code to leave your review:

If you feel good about helping someone you've never met, you are my kind of person. Welcome to the club. You're one of us.

I'm much more excited to help you achieve the best bucket list results, enjoy a longer Healthspan, and create more Memorable Experiences than you can imagine. You'll love all 5 of these POWERFUL STRATEGIES I will share with you.

Thank you from the bottom of my heart. Now, back to our regularly scheduled program.

  - Your biggest fan, Pete Bosse

P.S. - Fun fact: If you provide something of value to another person, it makes you more valuable to them. If you think this book will help someone you know, send it their way.

STRATEGY 3 - CREATING MEMORABLE EXPERIENCES

"Eat at a local restaurant tonight. Get the cream sauce. Have a cold pint at 4 o'clock in a mostly empty bar. Go somewhere you've never been. Listen to someone you think may have nothing in common with you. Order the steak rare. Eat an oyster. Have a Negroni. Have two. Be open to a world where you may not understand or agree with the person next to you, but have a drink with them anyways. Eat slowly. Tip your server. Check in on your friends. Check in on yourself. Enjoy the ride." [1]

ANTHONY BOURDAIN

Preparing for retirement involves more than setting aside money and making arrangements. It also entails exploring ways to create experiences that enhance your retirement years. *"We are such stuff as dreams are made on, and our little life is rounded with a sleep."* – Shakespeare, *The Tempest*. Picture waking up each morning excited, not for what the day may bring

---

1. https://www.facebook.com/photo.php?fbid=851119013793577&set

but for the thrilling adventure of checking off each item on your bucket list. This isn't just any list; it's a vibrant tapestry of dreams and ambitions woven over a lifetime now ripe for exploration with the enthusiasm of newfound freedom that retirement brings. This section will delve into how you can make the most of your retirement by crafting enduring memories. Let's explore some inspiring ideas and suggestions to help you embrace the retired life. *"Memories are time that you borrow, to spend when you get to tomorrow."* – Paul Anka.

3.1 CRAFTING YOUR ULTIMATE BUCKET LIST

Identifying Personal Dreams

The first step in crafting your ultimate bucket list begins with deep-diving into your aspirations. Remember when a book, a movie, or a casual conversation sparked a sudden flame where you said to yourself: 'I want to do that someday.' Now is your time to revisit those wishes. Whether it's the thrill of skydiving, the allure of learning a new language, or the simple joy of gardening, each desire has a place on your list. This exploration is about filling your days and enriching your life with experiences that resonate with your deepest passions and values. Reflect on what truly brings you joy and fulfillment. Is it adventure, knowledge, creativity, or tranquility? By aligning your bucket list with these core elements of your personality, you set the stage for experiences that are not only enjoyable but also profoundly meaningful.

Setting Achievable Goals

When setting goals, start by turning your dreams into objectives. Break down aspirations into steps to make them more attainable and manageable. For example, set writing targets if you aspire to write a novel. Sign up for a writing class. If travel is your passion, begin exploring destinations or save a fixed amount each month for trips. Consistency is required; small and steady progress leads to accomplishments. Setting timelines and considering your existing commitments and well-being is essential to ensure that pursuing your goals adds value to your life without causing stress. Remember, the bucket list isn't a sprint but a fulfilling journey.

Incorporating Variety

Variety is the spice of life, and this is especially true for your bucket list. Include a variety of experiences that cater to different aspects of your personality and interests. Mix in global adventures, physical and intellectual pursuits, and solo and social activities. For example, you could take a cooking class one month and go on a hiking trip the next. Balance a retreat for self-reflection with attending a lively cultural festival. This mix ensures that your activities stay engaging and appealing to all facets of who you are. It makes the journey of checking items off your bucket list as thrilling as the experiences.

Crafting your bucket list goes beyond listing fun things to do; it's about creating a roadmap for leading a fulfilling, vibrant life. It's about adding a touch of joy, learning, and adventure to your retirement years. Each dream on your list is a step toward experiences and uncovering aspects of yourself and the world around you. So let your imagination run wild, follow your dreams, and make each day in retirement a journey toward embracing life to the fullest.

Exercise 2. Create Your Bucket-List

1. Take out a blank sheet of paper.
2. Start by brainstorming everything you have wanted to do but have been putting off.
3. Organize the list by grouping similar things.
4. Now, consolidate the list with all travel in one category, for example, and like things together in other categories.
5. Next, prioritize that list based on your expected Healthspan and Finances.
6. Now you've got a prioritized Bucket-List!

Review and Adapt

Reviewing and adjusting your bucket list is crucial since it's a living document that should adapt to you. As your interests, abilities, and circumstances change, some goals may lose appeal while new ones emerge. Embrace this evolution. Keeping your bucket list up to date is part of the adventure. It reflects your growth and learning as you explore retirement further. You may have uncovered a talent for painting and developed a newfound passion for birdwatching. Let your list be flexible to accommodate your evolving passions and dreams.

> *Quick Tip: Enjoying experiences requires time, health, and money. More money doesn't get you more experience points since it is often a trade-off with time and health. Therefore, you should avoid chasing more money since no number will*

ever seem like enough, and invest your time and health in creating those memorable experiences.[2]

3.2 PLANNING YOUR RETIREMENT TRAVEL: TIPS AND DESTINATIONS

Travel can be one of the transformative aspects of retirement, exposing you to diverse landscapes, cultures, and experiences that expand your horizons and rejuvenate your soul. When planning your travel goals, consider what truly interests you and how it aligns with your capabilities. If exploring ruins excites you, do that. If tranquil scenery and peaceful towns suit you better, tailor your travel plans to ensure each trip is enjoyable and manageable based on your health and stamina levels. Think about destinations that have always captured your imagination or places that tug at your heartstrings for exploration or learning opportunities. Remember that exploring gems within your country can be just as exciting— and often less demanding—than far-flung destinations.

> *Quick Tip: Reflect on the three retirement phases I introduced in the Introduction section of this book. Remember to prioritize your list according to your expected Healthspan. At 70 or older, you're much less likely to be skydiving or climbing Mt. Everest.*

When you're planning your trips, budgeting is essential. Start by listing the expenses linked to your destinations, including travel costs, accommodation, meals, and activities. Planning allows you to benefit from discounts and special deals, which can significantly

---

2.   Perkins, B. J. (2020). *Die with zero: Getting all you can from your money and your life.* Boston, MA: Houghton Mifflin.

reduce expenses. Selecting the time to travel is crucial, too; going during off-peak seasons can save you money. Improve your experience by avoiding crowds. This strategy lets you enjoy a pace and form a deeper bond with the place you're visiting. Also, make a packing list customized for your destination and needs so you have all the essentials for comfort and convenience without over-packing.

> *Quick Tip: Check out last-minute travel sites for deep discounts on locations from your bucket list. Since many retirees have more flexibility regarding travel, these sites may offer incredible value opportunities.*

Getting involved with travel groups can be advantageous because they offer social connections and logistical support that enrich your travel adventures. These groups frequently organize tours tailored for seniors with considerations like pace, accessibility, and healthcare facilities in mind. Group travels also allow you to connect with individuals who share your enthusiasm for exploration and new experiences. The sense of camaraderie within these travel groups can transform a journey into an adventure filled with companionship and shared moments. Additionally, these groups often feature experienced guides who offer insights into the culture and history of the destinations, enhancing your understanding and appreciation of the places you explore.

> *Quick Tip: I'm a member of several organizations, and they always offer guided tours for members. These are a great way to meet new friends and relieve the burden of planning by leaving the details to the tour organization.*

When suggesting travel destinations for seniors, some options blend convenience with excitement. Within the USA, destinations like Sedona, Arizona, known for its viewing spots and picturesque landscapes, or Asheville, North Carolina, celebrated for its lively arts scene and senior-friendly activities, are worth considering. Internationally, countries such as New Zealand offer awe-inspiring scenery and structured tours catering to physical capabilities. Similarly, countries like Portugal boast distinctive landscapes. It has one of the most affordable living costs in Western Europe, making it an appealing choice for extended stays.

> *Quick Tip: Italy is a particular favorite of mine when vacationing. It offers excellent food and wine, incredible art and architecture, a robust history, friendly people, and spectacular landscapes and vistas. I once had a personal one-on-one guided tour of three Tuscan wineries when the rest of the tour group didn't show up.*

When traveling during retirement, it's vital to prioritize your health and safety. Ensure that insurance covers expenses and emergencies abroad since basic Medicare doesn't work internationally. Before your trip, consult your doctor to ensure you're healthy for travel and discuss any recommended vaccinations or medications. Keep a list of your medications with their names, as brands may vary in other countries. It's also essential to learn about the healthcare facilities at your destination to ensure access to care when needed. Being well-prepared is key to an enjoyable travel experience, allowing you to explore the world confidently and with peace of mind.

Quick Tip: I recently purchased a one-year travel policy from Allianz for less than $500. It has excellent health coverage and trip interruption coverage. If you are traveling more than a few times per year, it can be more cost-effective than purchasing insurance for each trip. Check out several providers to get the policy that's best for you.

3.3 THE JOY OF GRANDPARENTING: FUN THINGS TO DO WITH GRANDKIDS

Retirees who are much happier in their post-work years tend to engage in social activities such as spending time with loved ones, exercising, pursuing hobbies, and traveling.[3] Being a grandparent comes with its joys and blessings. It allows you to shape and enhance your grandchildren's lives while seeing the world anew through their perspective. The activities you engage in together can strengthen your bond. Create lasting memories that will be treasured for years to come. Adapting activities to suit age groups ensures that every moment spent together is enjoyable and contributes positively to their development and your relationship.

Engaging in play can be both educational and entertaining for children and toddlers. Activities such as molding dough, finger painting, or playing in a sandbox stimulate their senses and aid in developing motor skills. As children grow older, solving puzzles or sharing stories during story time can boost their abilities while allowing them to pass on tales or personal anecdotes, deepening their bond. For school-aged grandchildren, constructing model kits —whether it's cars, airplanes, or even basic robotics—can be an

---

3. https://www.thinkadvisor.com/2024/03/13/a-third-of-americans-are-not-happier-in-retirement-study/ , accessed on 9/08/24.

activity that also imparts valuable lessons in patience and problem-solving, encouraging teamwork and closeness.

Teenagers may find enjoyment in more intellectually stimulating pursuits. Spending quality time with your teenage grandchildren by playing their video games or going on nature walks and bird-watching excursions can be a fantastic way to educate them about the environment and the significance of conservation. This can ignite a passion for nature and science in them. Taking photography walks where each person has a camera to capture moments during the outing can also be quite engaging. It allows them to showcase their creativity and could even spark a hobby or interest.

Integrating elements into these activities enhances the time spent together. Visiting museums that cater to their interests, whether in science, art, or history, can be enjoyable and enlightening. Cooking classes are especially beneficial as they impart life skills while incorporating lessons in math and chemistry, all while creating dishes you can savor together. These experiences offer hands-on learning in an enjoyable atmosphere, making the education they gain memorable and valuable.

Establishing traditions with your grandchildren can provide them with consistency and security, knowing that certain things will remain constant despite any changes. Creating traditions like trips to a destination can become something they eagerly anticipate throughout the year, just as holiday customs such as baking cookies can bring joy and bonding moments. Crafting together, whether projects for little ones or more intricate creations for older kids, boosts creativity and builds a bank of shared memories and skills they carry with them as they grow.

Quick Tip: We took a few trips with our grandkids to Disneyworld in Florida when they were very young, and they still talk about it years later. Create great memories!

In today's era, maintaining bonds with grandchildren has become more accessible and impactful, thanks to technology. Engaging through video calls can significantly influence the quality of your relationship. Platforms like Zoom or Skype enable you to be part of their routines, whether virtually reading them bedtime stories or assisting with schoolwork. Online games and virtual reality experiences can also be enjoyed together from afar, allowing you to embark on adventures from your homes. Teaching them tech skills, helping them set up devices, and educating them about safety are lessons you can impart while making your interactions enjoyable and educational.

The role of a grandparent is wonderfully multifaceted and incredibly fulfilling.

It allows you to mentor, educate, and lead while enjoying, engaging, discovering, and being together. Every educational, artistic, or enjoyable activity nurtures your connections, creates enduring memories, and leaves behind a heritage of affection and wisdom that surpasses the moment's happiness. In the role of a grandparent, each shared moment is a thread woven into the fabric of a bond that carries the warmth and love of family through generations.

3.4 EXPLORING NEW PASSIONS AND HOBBIES

Retirement is a chapter of freedom, a time to indulge in activities that truly pique your interest. It's a fresh start, allowing you to nurture interests that may have been overlooked during your working years. Whether it's immersing yourself in arts and crafts, staying updated on the latest tech trends, enjoying the gameplay of pickleball, engaging in competition fishing, or taking on DIY home improvement projects, a wide range of hobbies is waiting to be explored.

The charm of hobbies lies in their joy and positive impact on your well-being. Participating in enjoyable activities can significantly boost your health by offering a break from routine and reducing stress levels. It expresses creativity, keeps your mind active, and continuously fosters learning – elements crucial for health as you age. Additionally, hobbies such as gardening, hiking, or playing pickleball can enhance your well-being by improving endurance, strength, and flexibility, contributing to a healthy lifestyle. From a broader perspective, hobbies provide an avenue for meeting new people or strengthening existing relationships by creating shared interests, bonding, and conversing.

> *Quick Tip: I learned how to play pickleball (America's fastest-growing sport, according to some) on a trip to Florida a few years ago, and I've been hooked ever since. We now have paddles and a net at home, so we can play in the driveway instead of driving to a court. It's invigorating and fun simultaneously.*

Finding suitable classes or groups where you can learn and enjoy hobbies with others adds an invaluable social dimension to your hobby pursuits. Many places like community centers, libraries, and colleges offer classes tailored to seniors' interests, ranging from pottery and photography workshops to computer courses and book clubs. These gatherings are about acquiring skills, sharing stories, making friends, and connecting with like-minded individuals.

Being part of groups offers structured interactions that can be particularly beneficial if you feel lonely or isolated.

Creating a space at home for your hobbies can significantly enhance your enjoyment and dedication to these activities. Design an inviting area where all your supplies are easily accessible; for instance, if painting is your passion, set up your easels and paints in a well-lit spot with natural light pouring in. Storing your supplies in labeled containers in a cozy area that beckons you to relax and unleash your creativity is helpful when pursuing a craft hobby. Ensure this space is tidy and free of distractions, creating a haven dedicated to inspiration and peace. This physical space makes engaging in your hobby more enjoyable and provides a visual reminder and motivator to spend time doing what you love.

By delving into hobbies, you're sowing the seeds of happiness that can flourish into blooms of satisfaction and self-discovery during your retirement years. Each hobby you explore opens pathways for growth, knowledge, and contentment, enriching your life immeasurably. Whether crafting, playing games, or acquiring skills, approaching these pursuits with enthusiasm and curiosity will aid in integrating them as beloved parts of your daily routine.

3.5 FAMILY REUNIONS AND CREATING NEW TRADITIONS

There is something magical about bringing together multiple generations in one place, sharing tales and laughter that linger long after everyone has dispersed to their respective corners of the world. Organizing and participating in family gatherings that capture this enchantment and cater to people of all ages require thoughtful consideration and a sprinkle of imagination; it all starts by deeply understanding the dynamics of your family and considering each member's age, interests, and requirements. This insight will help you choose activities that engage everyone, ensuring no one feels excluded. For example, while youngsters enjoy outdoor games, older folks may prefer quieter pursuits like card games or storytelling sessions.

When picking a location, consider accessibility for all attendees, including those with mobility issues. Opting for a venue that's easy to navigate ensures that everyone feels at ease and included. Additionally, think about the amenities and accommodation options that can meet the varied needs of a large group—and plan your gathering when most family members are likely free, perhaps during summer holidays for school children or over weekends. This increases the chances of more relatives being able to join in on the fun. A shared digital calendar can help coordinate schedules and organize events.

> *Quick Tip: I recently returned from a family reunion in Michigan. The facility at Pioneer Park, north of Muskegon, was a sturdy log cabin pavilion that seated up to 100 people at picnic tables. About 70 relatives attended, and we all had a great time. Contribute time, energy, and funds to make the event successful for all attending. Take lots of pictures!*

Introducing new traditions during reunions can strengthen familial bonds and create lasting memories. Traditions could range from activities like taking a family portrait or conducting a reunion fundraising auction to more elaborate ones such as hosting a family Olympics with various entertaining games for all generations. Another delightful tradition could involve creating a 'time capsule' where each family member contributes something from their year to be opened at a reunion. These traditions often become the highlights of our gatherings, eagerly anticipated and cherished by every family member.

> *Quick Tip: My wife's family held an annual gathering called Spanfest, since their last name is Spaniol, for nearly a decade when all the kids were young, and we all have the most beautiful memories of these fun events and the pool volleyball challenges.*

Technology plays a crucial role in organizing successful family reunions. Online tools and applications make it easier to plan the event, from scheduling activities to deciding on the menu. Platforms like Google Sheets or Trello enable family members to share ideas, volunteer for tasks, and stay updated on real-time planning progress. Additionally, technology helps bridge gaps during these reunions, ensuring that nobody is left out and everyone feels included. Presenting a family game that provides questions spanning various decades can offer an enjoyable opportunity for younger members to delve into their heritage and for older members to share their personal stories.

> *Quick Tip: Check out Mentimeter.com, an interactive app that allows users to ask questions and share real-time anonymous responses using colorful graphics. During the COVID lockdown, we used this and Zoom to stay in touch and engage with others.*

Moreover, for families spread across the globe, technology ensures that no one misses out. Live streaming parts of the reunion or having a virtual 'guest book' where distant family members can leave video messages are beautiful ways to include everyone. These tools help manage the logistics of such gatherings and enhance the experience, making it easier and more enjoyable for everyone involved. The key is to leverage technology as a tool for organization and as a bridge that connects family members, weaving their individual stories into the rich tapestry of family history.

In planning these gatherings, remember that the goal is not perfection but connection. It's about creating a space where family members, separated by geography and the hustle of daily life, can reconnect and make new memories. It's about celebrating the legacy of the past while embracing the promise of the future together as one family.

3.6 ENGAGING WITH LOCAL AND GLOBAL COMMUNITIES

Enhancing the tapestry of your retirement involves pursuing personal growth activities in solitude and immersing yourself in vibrant communities. Picture strolling through the streets of a festival, feeling the pulse of community spirit with each step, or experiencing deep satisfaction by supporting global causes that resonate with your values. Connecting with international communities expands your worldview and fosters a sense of belonging and purpose that brings profound fulfillment.

Taking part in community gatherings such as festivals, charity functions, and cultural events offers a chance to remain involved and connected within your community. These occasions provide opportunities to meet individuals, discover cultures, and share experiences that enrich your social circle. Volunteering at a neighborhood food distribution event or attending a community art showcase supports your community. It also adds layers of significance to your social connections, making your retirement life as rich in relationships as it is in personal time.

Quick Tip: I grew up in Michigan and always enjoyed the summer there. I especially enjoyed Yankee Doodle Days in our small town in June every year. This community festival included artwork, bands, parades, and local shops selling items on the street. It was fun and exciting, and the roads were always crowded. This gathering provided fond memories as our family engaged with the community each year.

Volunteering abroad represents a unique intersection of travel and altruism, offering a path to contribute to global communities while experiencing new cultures significantly. Programs like Peace Corps for older adults or various NGO initiatives designed for senior volunteers provide structured opportunities to help on projects that range from education in underdeveloped countries to conservation efforts in endangered ecosystems. This kind of involvement not only leaves a positive footprint on the world but also immerses you in new cultural experiences that are both humbling and enriching, offering perspectives that challenge and grow your worldview.

Quick Tip: Organizations like Crossroads Africa offer opportunities for small groups to volunteer for projects overseas. I'm a 1979 participant, and our group raised funds and went to Mali to photograph architectural monuments for the Ministry of Antiquities. They always look for mature adults to be volunteer group guides each summer.

Joining special interest groups can be particularly rewarding, allowing you to connect with like-minded individuals who share your passions. Whether it's a gardening club that meets weekly to share tips and seeds, a book club that gathers to dissect the latest literary masterpiece, or a travel club that plans annual adventures, these groups provide social interactions that can be intellectually and emotionally rewarding. The shared enthusiasm in these groups promotes a sense of community and belonging that is essential at any stage of life, particularly during retirement when forging new social connections can be more challenging.

Community education programs offer another avenue for growth and interaction. Many local colleges, libraries, and community centers provide courses on various subjects—from history to technology, arts to science. These classes allow you to dive into new knowledge areas and meet people of all ages and backgrounds, enriching your social circle. Engaging in educational programs can transform learning into an interactive, communal experience that expands your knowledge and social interactions, weaving learning seamlessly into the social aspects of your life.

Engaging with your local or global community opens new avenues for connection and contribution, making every interaction a thread in the larger social tapestry of your retirement. Whether through participation in local events, volunteering abroad, joining interest groups, or enrolling in community education, each activity you choose enriches your retirement experience, making it as socially fulfilling as it is personally gratifying.

3.7 THE PLEASURES OF EXPLORING CUISINE AND COOKING

Venturing into the world of exploration during retirement goes beyond passing the time; it's about adding excitement to your life with new flavors and experiences that please your taste buds and nourish your body. Cooking evolves from a task into a journey, where each ingredient opens up possibilities. I urge you to enter the kitchen with a spirit of discovery, eager to experiment with recipes and cuisines you may not have had the chance to explore.

Trying dishes from different cultures can be especially exciting. Picture bringing the flavors of trattorias or the lively street food of Bangkok into your kitchen. Start easy—with a dish that caught your attention during your travels or one you've come across in a book or on a cooking show. Exploring tastes and mastering recipes can be highly satisfying and are great ways to enhance your culinary abilities while immersing yourself in global cultures without leaving home. Each new recipe is a tale to enjoy and discuss, like an adventure.

Take cooking classes to improve your skills and connect with fellow food enthusiasts. Many local community centers, culinary schools, and even certain restaurants provide classes tailored to interests and proficiency levels. Exploring the art of making sushi or diving into Mediterranean cuisine's flavors during a class can broaden your cooking skills. These classes often wrap up with everyone enjoying a meal, offering a great chance to make new friends and savor the delicious dishes you've prepared in good company.

> *Quick Tip: We have taken cooking classes at Central Market in San Antonio five or six times. The classes are always fantastic. We learn how to create fun and tasty dishes while enjoying a few glasses of wine. The social element of meeting new people is an additional bonus.*

Hosting gatherings centered around cooking can transform your home into a hub for socializing. Think about throwing theme-inspired cooking parties where each guest brings a themed dish or potluck events where the only rule is to bring something. These get-togethers could also be an opportunity to share family recipes or experiment with ones that might become traditions in your family kitchen. Cooking together fosters a bond, making the dining experience more delightful. It's about creating an environment where laughter and stories flow freely as the food passes around the table.

> *Quick Tip: My favorite hosted cooking experience was at a friend's house, where we learned how to make Chinese potstickers from scratch. This is an excellent way to get together with friends, rotate the location, and learn something new while enjoying each other's company. (There may have been some wine served, too!)*

Eating well becomes even more crucial as we age, and cooking at home allows you to control the quality and quantity of ingredients in your meals. Focus on delicious recipes and cooking methods that benefit your health. Add plenty of vegetables, whole grains, and lean proteins to your dishes to maintain a balanced diet. Cooking methods like steaming, grilling, or baking are healthier alternatives to frying and can be just as flavorful with the right herbs and spices. Remember, healthy cooking does not have to be bland—the abundance of spices and herbs from different cuisines worldwide can turn nutritious meals into exquisite culinary experiences.

As you explore the joys of culinary exploration and cooking, remember that each meal you prepare expresses creativity and care. It's a delightful dance of flavors and textures that satisfies the palate and nurtures the body and soul. Whether you're cooking for one, a family, or a house full of guests, the kitchen can be a place of endless discovery and joy. So, don your apron with excitement, wield your spatula with confidence, and let the magic of cooking enrich your retirement years!

3.8 HOME PROJECTS: RENOVATIONS AND GARDENING

Engaging in home improvement projects can bring a sense of fulfillment as you transform your living space into a practical sanctuary that reflects your lifestyle and boosts your property's worth. When planning renovations, it's necessary to combine your vision with practicality. Start by identifying areas in your home that could use updates or changes to meet your needs better. Perhaps the kitchen requires a user layout for easier cooking, or the bathroom could benefit from safety additions like grab bars and a walk-in shower. Prioritizing these projects based on their impact on your comfort and home value can help direct your focus.

When mapping out renovations, consider the long-term advantages of each project. For example, improving your home's insulation enhances energy efficiency and reduces heating and cooling expenses. Similarly, installing windows can boost light, creating a brighter and more welcoming atmosphere while decreasing reliance on artificial lighting. Consider incorporating home technology as well. Features like smart thermostats, lighting systems, and security devices can facilitate convenience and safety in your living space. These innovations allow you to easily control aspects of your home through voice commands or simple touches.

> *Quick Tip: I installed smart thermostats and a solar-powered attic fan and added multi-layer insulation, and my heating and cooling bills have decreased by 20% per year.*

Gardening opens the gate to the serenity of nature in your backyard. This therapeutic and physically rewarding activity is an effective way to keep active. Embarking on your gardening journey can be an exploration into the realm of plants. Choose a spot with sunlight and good soil quality. Start small by growing easy-to-care-for plants, which can build your confidence to expand your garden gradually. Herbs like basil, mint, and parsley are choices for beginners who want to add flavors to their culinary creations. Growing vegetables such as tomatoes, cucumbers, and peppers can also be fulfilling, allowing you to savor the satisfaction of harvesting your homegrown produce.

The benefits of your garden go beyond the pleasure of harvesting produce. The physical exertion of gardening can enhance your endurance, strength, and flexibility. Planting, weeding, and watering are ways to keep moving without putting strain on your body. The tranquility and contentment derived from caring for your plants can significantly reduce stress levels and contribute to well-being. To improve your gardening experience, use raised beds or try container gardening. These methods can help make gardening more manageable by reducing the need for bending and stooping.

> *Quick Tip: In his book Blue Zones, Dan Buettner discusses the importance of gardening and how people in all five Blue Zones continue to garden well into their 90s and 100s.*[4] *Gardening is an enriching activity at any age.*

Safety and ergonomic design are crucial to ensuring injury-free activities for home renovations and gardening. When renovating your home, consider designs that minimize strain and improve accessibility. Features like lever door handles, non-slip flooring, and pull-out cabinets can significantly enhance your daily comfort. Similarly, using tools to reduce effort and strain can make

---

4. Buettner, D. (2017). *The blue zones of happiness: Lessons from the world's happiest people.* Washington, D.C.: National Geographic.

gardening a pleasant experience. Tools with handles and easy grip designs can help prevent hand and back strain while making gardening more accessible.

Choosing eco-friendly home improvements is beneficial for your home and the environment. Consider investing in energy-efficient appliances, solar panels, or green roofing systems to lower your carbon footprint and save money on utility bills. In your garden, consider composting kitchen scraps, harvesting rainwater for irrigation, and using mulches to enrich the soil and support healthier plant growth without relying on chemicals.

Through thoughtful planning and execution, home projects like renovations and gardening can significantly enhance your quality of life, providing a safe, comfortable, and enjoyable living environment. These activities adapt your home to meet your evolving needs better and offer rewarding pastimes that enrich your retirement years with purpose and joy. Whether updating your home to suit your lifestyle better or cultivating a garden for beauty and sustenance, each project can transform your living space into a more personalized and fulfilling environment.

3.9 STAYING ACTIVE WITH SPORTS AND OUTDOOR ACTIVITIES

While most pre-retirees had planned an active retirement filled with travel and exercise, 83% of current retirees reported watching TV as their top activity.[5] Participating in sports and outdoor activities can significantly enhance your retirement experience. It brings advantages and the pleasure of connecting with nature and the community. Sports catering to various fitness levels and age

5. https://www.thinkadvisor.com/2024/03/13/a-third-of-americans-are-not-happier-in-retirement-study/ , accessed on 9/08/24.

groups, such as golf, swimming, pickleball, and yoga, are highlighted for their versatility and advantages. Golf, for example, offers a mix of activity and social engagement, allowing you to relish the outdoors while partaking in a sport that demands precision and strategic thinking. Swimming is an option for those seeking an intense yet equally fulfilling workout regimen. It is especially beneficial for individuals dealing with problems like arthritis since the water buoyancy alleviates strain on the body while delivering an exercise session.

Pickleball, which merges elements from tennis, badminton, and table tennis into a paddle sport, is rapidly gaining popularity among adults. It's enjoyable. It serves as a method to enhance hand-eye coordination and reflexes with a reduced risk of injury. Yoga is renowned for its poses promoting stress relief; it can be particularly advantageous for improving flexibility, balance, and mental well-being.

It's easy to adjust these activities to suit your comfort and fitness levels, making them a flexible choice for staying healthy as you age. Engaging in these activities regularly offers health benefits. Physical activity helps maintain and enhance mobility to preserve independence with age. Activities like swimming and cycling can significantly boost health, lowering the risk of heart disease and stroke. Exercise also positively impacts mental well-being as it releases endorphins, the body's natural mood enhancers, which can help alleviate feelings of depression and anxiety.

Additionally, participating in sports or clubs can improve your mood and reduce loneliness concerns in later stages of life. This flexibility empowers you to take control of your health and well-being, making your retirement years more fulfilling. Being part of clubs or sports leagues goes beyond activity; they foster community bonds and social interactions that contribute to your well-being alongside exercise. Local clubs often offer training sessions, competitive games, and social gatherings that create a schedule of engaging activities to keep you connected. Whether you join a golf league or a swimming club or attend a yoga class in your area, being part of a group helps you stay committed and motivated to keep active. Connecting with individuals can form new friendships and social circles, offering opportunities for engaging in various physical activities, classes, and hobbies. This sense of community can make you feel connected and engaged, enhancing your retirement experience.

> *Quick Tip: Some active senior communities, like Del Webb, offer an array of physical activities, classes, and hobbies to keep members engaged, active, and social in support of their longevity.*

Pursuits like hiking, bird watching, or cycling promote physical fitness and allow for a deeper connection with nature, which can be incredibly revitalizing. Exploring parks or nature reserves through hiking offers a way to appreciate the natural surroundings at your own pace. Tailoring the length and difficulty of hikes to suit your fitness level while immersing yourself in the sights and sounds of nature—birdsong, lush greenery, scents—can positively impact mental health and general wellness. Bird watching allows one to enjoy the outdoors while pursuing a gratifying hobby. Whether on a bicycle or an e-bike, cycling enables you to explore distances outdoors, reaping cardiovascular benefits and experiencing the thrill of discovery.

Embracing these activities enhances physical and mental health and enriches your life with new skills, friendships, and experiences. It transforms staying active from a chore into a joyful discovery and connection-filled pursuit. Whether perfecting your swing on the golf course, mastering the art of a yoga pose, or exploring a beautiful trail, each activity you engage in adds a rich layer to your retirement.

3.10 CONNECTED TECHNOLOGY: EASY AND SIMPLE TOOLS FOR ADULTS 50+

Navigating the digital world can seem daunting, but embracing technology can significantly enhance your ability to stay connected with loved ones and keep up with the world around you. Let's start with the basics: user-friendly devices such as smartphones, tablets, and straightforward apps. These tools are designed with intuitive interfaces, meaning you don't have to be a tech wizard to benefit from them. A smartphone or tablet can be your gateway to staying informed, entertained, and, most importantly, connected with family and friends. The trick is to choose devices that prioritize ease of use—look for those with large displays and straightforward navigation.

Social media platforms like Facebook, Instagram, and WhatsApp have revolutionized how we connect, allowing us to maintain relationships across miles and time zones with just a few clicks. Starting with Facebook, it's a fantastic platform for staying updated on the lives of your family and friends. You can share updates and photos and participate in groups that align with your interests. Instagram allows more visual interaction, where you can enjoy pictures and videos from loved ones or share your own. WhatsApp provides a streamlined, secure way to send messages, make voice calls, and even video calls, making it incredibly useful for real-time communication, and it's free!

Video communication tools have become essential, especially if family members live far away or you cannot visit friends as often as you'd like. Applications such as Skype, Zoom, and FaceTime are invaluable for this purpose. They allow you to hear and see your loved ones, sharing moments as if together in the same room. Whether you're witnessing a grandchild's first steps or celebrating a birthday together, these tools ensure you are part of the moments that matter. Setting up these applications might seem complicated, but their ease of use will become clear once you step through the initial setup.

However, with the increased use of technology comes the need for vigilance against potential online threats. Please try to understand the basics of online safety to protect yourself from scams and privacy breaches. Always use strong, unique passwords for different sites, avoid sharing sensitive information like your social security number or financial details online, and be wary of unsolicited emails or messages that ask for personal info. Regularly updating your software and applications can also help protect you from security vulnerabilities. These practices aren't just prudent but necessary to ensure your digital adventures remain safe and enjoyable.

> *Quick Tip: Remember how my 85-year-old dad was the victim of a phishing scam by inadvertently clicking on a suspicious link in an email? I highly recommend virus protection software for everyone. Please DO NOT click on something without virus protection.*

By embracing these technologies, you can combat feelings of loneliness that sometimes accompany aging and bridge the gap between generations. You become part of a community where you can share, learn, and grow. This keeps your mind active and enhances your relationships, fostering ways of connecting and understanding with your loved ones. Let's embrace this journey together, turning any fears into excitement about the opportunities modern technology brings to strengthen our bonds and enrich our lives.

As we conclude this discussion on using technology to stay connected, it's evident that the digital realm offers more than convenience—a solid link to our family and community. Whether learning about user devices, navigating social media platforms, utilizing video communication tools, or ensuring safety, each aspect significantly improves our interactions and safeguards our online presence. Remember that technology is more than a tool; it acts as a gateway to nurturing and fostering relationships, delving into hobbies, and engaging actively in our ever-growing, interconnected society.

STRATEGY 4 - BUILDING RESILIENCE

BOUNCING BACK FROM ADVERSITY

"Be flexible like trees; when the wind blows, bend, but do not break." [1]

MATSHONA DHLIWAYO

W hen Martha first retired, she envisaged endless days of relaxation and hobbies she never had time for. Barely a year later, however, she felt unexpectedly unmoored, realizing that her professional life had provided more than just income—it had given her structure, purpose, and a sense of belonging. While filled with potential, this new chapter also brought significant life changes, and adapting wasn't as straightforward as she had hoped. Martha's journey to finding resilience in retirement is a testament to the power and necessity of embracing adaptability and strength during this phase of life. I'm fond of the book *Everything is*

1. Dhliwayo, M. (n.d.). Quotefancy. Retrieved from https://quotefancy.com/quote/3544792/Matshona-Dhliwayo-Be-flexible-like-trees-when-life-s-winds-blow-bend-but-do-not-break , accessed on 7/11/24.

Figureoutable by Marie Forleo, where she notes that sometimes, figuring things out requires that you refuse to be refused and disagree with someone else's view of reality - you should question the rules.[2]

4.1 RESILIENCE TRAINING: TECHNIQUES FOR ADAPTING TO CHANGE

Understanding Resilience in the Context of Aging

Resilience, in its essence, is about bouncing back from challenges and adapting to change. It's about facing life's upheavals, not just enduring them, but emerging more robust and resourceful. For retirees like Martha, resilience is crucial. As Albert Einstein said, "You never fail until you stop trying." Stoicism began over 2000 years ago and centers on the idea that people should focus only on what they can control and ignore what they cannot. The shift from a structured work life to the freedom of retirement can be disorienting, affecting one's identity and sense of worth. Health issues might arise, financial realities can hurt, and the loss of social connections can profoundly impact mental health. Building resilience helps you navigate these changes, ensuring your retirement years are about survival, thriving, and a renewed sense of self.

Building Resilience Skills

One effective technique for cultivating resilience is cognitive reframing. This involves changing negative patterns of thinking

---

2. Forleo, M. (2019). *Everything is figureoutable*. USA: Penguin Random House LLC.

into more positive, adaptive thoughts. For instance, rather than viewing retirement as the end of your productive years, you can see it as an opportunity to explore passions and activities you were previously too busy to consider. Emotional regulation is another helpful skill, helping you manage feelings of anxiety or sadness that might arise with significant life changes. Techniques such as deep breathing exercises, mindfulness, and meditation can aid significantly in maintaining emotional balance.

> *Quick Tip: I like viewing life as a metaphor, like a book you are continually writing. Each chapter is yours to write and make as long as you want. But eventually, you will close that chapter and start a new one. It's OK to have feelings about that closure as long as they are balanced with the excitement of starting the next chapter.*

Practicing realistic optimism involves acknowledging the realities of aging while also maintaining a hopeful outlook on what can be achieved. It's about setting attainable goals that bring genuine satisfaction and boost your sense of accomplishment. For example, if you loved marathon running in your younger years, shifting to shorter races or brisk walking can provide a sense of achievement that aligns better with your current physical capabilities. Also, consider transitioning from individual running to group walking, where you enjoy the benefits of developing relationships with fellow walkers while still getting your exercise.

Learning from Setbacks

Every challenge or setback is a reservoir of learning opportunities. Adopting this mindset is vital in building resilience. When plans fall through—maybe a planned trip gets canceled, or a hobby class doesn't turn out as enjoyable as expected—rather than dwelling on disappointment, focus on what these experiences teach you about your interests and adaptability. Perhaps the canceled trip opens the opportunity for incredibly fulfilling local explorations. Embracing flexibility allows you to navigate retirement with an open mind, making adjustments that enrich your life rather than constrain it.

> *Quick Tip: Try to turn lemons into lemonade. My wife and I stood in a three-hour line in Amsterdam to get through customs, fearing we would miss our cruise's departure. So we started talking to the people in front of us who were literally in (on) the same boat. We became best friends throughout our cruise and have remained good friends because we initiated a conversation.*

Resilience Through Physical Health

The physical aspect of resilience cannot be overstated. Chapter 1 discussed how regular exercise, adequate nutrition, and sufficient sleep are foundational to maintaining physical and mental health. However, in this section, we will expand on how physical activity, in particular, is a potent stress reliever and mood booster. Establishing a routine that includes walking, swimming, or yoga can improve cardiovascular health, enhance flexibility, and strengthen muscles, all contributing to overall resilience. Nutrition also plays a vital role—eating a balanced diet rich in fruits, vegetables, lean proteins, and whole grains fuels the body and mind, supporting cognitive function and energy levels. Lastly, never underestimate the power of good sleep. Quality rest rejuvenates the body and mind, equipping you to face each new day with vigor and vitality. According to the National Institutes of Health (NIH), sleep plays a vital role in good health and well-being throughout your life, and getting inadequate sleep over time can raise your risk of chronic (long-term) health problems.[3] Experts recommend that adults sleep between 7 and 9 hours a night.[4]

Martha's realization that resilience is not inherent but can be developed was a turning point in her retirement. By adopting these strategies, she found the strength to adapt to her new life phase and the courage to redefine it, embracing changes that brought new friendships, renewed purposes, and unanticipated joys. Like Martha, you too can see each day of your retirement not as a challenge to be endured but as an opportunity for growth and discovery, building a resilient spirit that embraces change with optimism and grace. Your good health can be a reservoir of strength that can be called upon to help you get through the toughest of times.

4.2 PREPARING YOUR BODY FOR AGING

The cornerstone of a vibrant retirement is undoubtedly your health. Maintaining physical resilience enhances your ability to enjoy life fully and fortifies you against the potential challenges that aging naturally brings. Imagine playing with your grandchildren in the park, traveling to new places without undue fatigue, or engaging in your favorite hobbies; these are the joys that robust physical health can continue to offer as you age.

---

3. https://www.nhlbi.nih.gov/health/sleep/why-sleep-important#:~:text=During%20sleep%2C%20your%20body%20is,long%2Dterm)%20health%20problems. , accessed on 7/30/24.

4. https://www.nhlbi.nih.gov/health/sleep/how-much-sleep   , accessed on 9/11/24.

Importance of Physical Resilience

Physical resilience goes beyond freedom from illness; it's about cultivating a body supporting your desired lifestyle. This form of resilience becomes increasingly significant as we age because our bodies naturally undergo changes that can impact everything from our bone density to our muscular strength and cardiovascular health. By prioritizing physical resilience, you enhance your quality of life and reduce the risk of falls, injuries, and illnesses compromising your independence and well-being. As Dr. Peter Attia noted in his book *Outlive, The Science and Art of Longevity*, exercise is our most potent tool for preventing cognitive decline.[5]

> *Quick Tip: Imagine dealing with a highly stressful situation such as selling your home, moving, and buying a new, smaller home. If you are frail or ill, how much more difficult would that be than if you were in good physical health?*

Preventative Health Practices

Routine practices and exercises to prevent injury and manage age-related physical decline are essential to safeguard your physical health. Regular strength training, for example, can help maintain muscle mass and bone density, which are crucial for mobility and preventing osteoporosis. Flexibility exercises such as yoga or stretching routines can improve your range of motion and decrease the risk of muscle strains and joint pain. It's also beneficial to incorporate balance exercises into your routine; activities like Tai

---

5.   Attia, P., Outlive, The Science and Art of Longevity, 2023, Penguin Random House, UK.

Chi or simple balance drills can significantly reduce your risk of falls, which are a leading cause of injury among older adults.

Cardiovascular health is another essential area that requires attention. Engaging in aerobic activities such as brisk walking, cycling, or swimming can help maintain heart health, improve circulation, and boost lung function. These activities help manage weight, reduce the risk of chronic diseases such as type 2 diabetes and heart disease, and can even improve mental health by reducing anxiety and depression. It's about finding activities you enjoy that can be incorporated regularly into your lifestyle, thus setting the foundation for sustained physical health.

Adaptive Exercises

Only some people can engage in high-impact activities, especially if dealing with chronic health issues like arthritis or heart conditions. This is where adaptive exercises come into play. These are modified activities designed to fit your specific health needs and physical limitations, helping you remain active without risking your health. For instance, chair yoga is an excellent alternative for those who find traditional yoga challenging. Water aerobics is another perfect option, providing the resistance needed for muscle strengthening while being gentle on the joints.

Working with a physical therapist or a certified fitness instructor who understands the nuances of training older adults can be invaluable. They can tailor an exercise program that addresses your specific health concerns, mobility limitations, and fitness level, ensuring your routine promotes safe and effective resilience.

Nutritional Support

Your diet plays a pivotal role in supporting physical resilience. Your nutritional needs change as you age, and your diet should adapt to meet these new demands. Adequate intake of essential nutrients such as calcium and vitamin D is crucial for bone health, while proteins are necessary for maintaining muscle mass. Antioxidant-rich foods, including fruits and vegetables, help combat inflammation and support immune function, which is vital for overall health and well-being.

> *Quick Tip: Based on Tony Robbins's book Lifeforce and advice from doctors at MyLifeforce.com, my supplements now include magnesium, taurine, methylation, and NMN, in addition to a 50+ multivitamin. I recommend consulting your medical doctor before taking any supplements.*

Staying hydrated is also crucial, something frequently missed out on, considering its importance in aging individuals' health and well-being levels deteriorating over time; this can cause water retention issues and reduced awareness of thirst, leading to a likelihood of dehydration problems down the line. Ensuring you drink fluids is crucial in supporting proper kidney function and keeping body temperature in check while enhancing the quality of your sleep routine. You should consume eight glasses of water daily to adequately meet your body's hydration needs.

Eating natural foods like fruits and vegetables, lean proteins, and whole grains while cutting down on sugary processed foods and unhealthy fats can significantly improve your body's strength and stamina. It's worth considering seeking guidance from a nutritionist who can offer tailored recommendations to suit your unique health requirements and lifestyle choices.

Taking care of your body with the kind of exercise and activities that suit you and eating well-balanced meals consistently will boost your readiness to tackle the changes that come with aging. It also guarantees that you can make the most of your later years, filled with energy and active involvement in life experiences to the fullest extent possible, with enthusiasm and a positive outlook.

4.3 EMOTIONAL RESILIENCE: ADAPTING TO LOSS AND CHANGE

Emotional resilience might be likened to a deeply rooted tree, able to sway with the strong winds of change and loss without breaking. In the context of aging, this resilience becomes crucial as you face inevitable crises, such as the loss of loved ones, health changes, or the end of a career that once defined you. Emotional resilience helps you navigate these waters, survive the storms, and emerge with new wisdom and strength.

Understanding emotional resilience involves recognizing it as the ability to mentally or emotionally cope with a crisis or quickly return to pre-crisis status. Resilience doesn't mean you won't experience difficulty or distress or that you're impervious to suffering. Rather, it signifies a commitment to finding a way through tough times, equipped with an understanding that these experiences can be transformative. For many, retirement is a profound transition, marked not just by a change in daily routines but also by an evolution in identity and social roles. The importance of emotional resilience lies in its capacity to help you adapt to these changes, maintaining your well-being and enabling you to continue engaging with life in meaningful ways.

Developing coping strategies is integral to nurturing your emotional resilience. One effective method is cultivating mindfulness, which involves paying attention to the present moment without judgment. By learning to pay attention to what's happening in front of us, we gain more than the sensations of life; we also increase our ability to act...being present is what makes that possible.[6] Mindfulness can decrease the impact of stressors by enhancing your response to challenges, allowing you to notice stress reactions without becoming overwhelmed by them. Techniques such as guided imagery, where you visualize a peaceful setting or a successful outcome to a challenging situation, can also encourage emotional relief and reframe your perspective on stressors. Another powerful strategy is to write in a journal, which can help process emotions and clarify thoughts. This self-expression provides a unique opportunity to vent frustrations and fears in a safe, private space, which can be particularly therapeutic during significant life transitions.

> *Quick Tip: I find writing a letter to someone who has wronged me (but never sending it) is an effective way to vent and get the frustration out on paper. For some reason, writing is an excellent release of all that mental angst.*

The role of support systems in building emotional resilience must be addressed. Networks, composed of family, friends, or interest-based groups, can give emotional comfort and practical help in times of need. They also offer a sense of belonging and purpose, vital for maintaining mental health. Regularly engaging with supportive individuals can boost your mood, distract you from

---

6. Waldinger, R., & Schulz, M. (2023). *The good life*. New York, NY: Simon & Schuster.

personal grief, and offer new insights and advice. In building these networks, reciprocating support is essential, strengthening bonds and ensuring a mutual exchange of care and attention. Community or spiritual groups can provide a sense of family and continuity for those lacking immediate family connections. Additionally, online platforms connect you with others with similar experiences or interests, expanding your support network beyond geographical limits.

> *Quick Tip: The Prostate Cancer Foundation (PCF) offers an excellent Facebook support group for those with a cancer diagnosis. Many organizations around the world provide similar support systems for those in need of emotional support.*

It's important to consider seeking professional help when your usual coping methods and support network aren't sufficient to handle life challenges. Trained professionals such as counselors or therapists possess the expertise to introduce approaches for handling grief and adjusting to changes in life situations. They can also assist in addressing feelings of depression or anxiety that may manifest due to these circumstances. In a setting with them, you may feel more at ease discussing emotions you wouldn't usually share with friends or family. Moreover, they can work with you to create coping strategies that suit your unique needs. Recognizing the importance of seeking support is vital. Indications could be enduring feelings of sadness or despair and anxiety that interfere with daily tasks. Taking action can help avoid more serious mental health challenges in the future, leading to faster healing and improved results overall.

When you work on strengthening your resilience, remember it's not just about avoiding sadness or setbacks but preparing yourself to confront and learn from these moments and ultimately grow personally. It's about mastering the ups and downs of life with poise and determination, knowing that every obstacle also opens doors for self-improvement and gaining deeper insights. As you evolve and flourish through these challenges, you accumulate a wealth of knowledge and bravery that enhances your existence and motivates and stands by others in your community.

4.4 FINANCIAL RESILIENCE: BUFFERING AGAINST ECONOMIC DOWNTURNS

Essentials of Financial Resilience

Imagine you're setting out for a long, adventurous expedition. Would you begin without ensuring you have enough provisions, a map, and perhaps some emergency supplies? Financial resilience is somewhat similar, but navigating through your retirement years is about having a robust financial plan that provides stability and confidence, allowing you to enjoy your retirement without worrying about economic downturns. Financial resilience involves creating a buffer that can sustain you through unexpected financial storms, whether personal emergencies or broader economic downturns. This resilience directly impacts your ability to maintain a comfortable lifestyle, manage healthcare costs, and provide for unforeseen needs. We will cover this topic in much more detail in the next chapter. But here are a few pieces of information related to building resilience.

Diversification of Assets

One of the foundational strategies for achieving financial resilience is the diversification of assets. Diversification isn't just a buzzword; it's a practical approach to managing risk and ensuring that your investments can endure through market volatility and economic downturns. Think of it as not putting all your eggs in one basket. If one investment decreases in value, another might increase or stabilize, balancing the overall impact on your portfolio. This can include a mix of stocks, bonds, real estate, and other investments tailored to your risk tolerance and retirement timeline. Diversification helps smooth out the risks and can provide more consistent returns over time. It's about preparing your financial portfolio to handle the ups and downs of the market, ensuring that your retirement funds remain secure and continue to grow. A Certified Financial Planner ® Professional can significantly help you as a fiduciary who acts in your best interest.

Emergency Funds

Another key component of financial resilience is maintaining an emergency fund. This fund is a financial safety net designed to cover unexpected expenses such as home repairs, medical emergencies, or sudden personal crises that might force you to dip into your retirement savings. This fund provides peace of mind and ensures you can handle surprises without jeopardizing your long-term financial plans. It's advisable to have enough in your emergency fund to cover three to six months of living expenses. This fund should be easily accessible, perhaps in a savings account, where you can withdraw the money without significant penalties or risks.

Quick Tip: An emergency fund is a colossal stress reliever. Never again will you let circumstances cause you stress and anguish when a few hundred or a few thousand dollars could eliminate the stress by tapping your emergency fund.

Staying Informed

Keeping up to date on current events is essential for maintaining stability and security in a world of constantly shifting economic conditions and regulations. Being informed about market trends and staying current on changes to tax laws and investment tactics plays a role in shaping your financial choices and the success of your retirement savings. Engaging with news sources regularly, signing up for expert advice services, and attending educational events, like workshops and seminars, are vital ways to stay informed. Additionally, a financial advisor's guidance could prove highly beneficial in navigating these complex financial landscapes. They offer custom advice that suits your circumstances and assist you in adapting your financial strategy accordingly while supporting you to make well-informed choices that strengthen your financial stability.

Establishing and sustaining stability isn't merely about safe-guarding your wealth; it's also about building a safety net that enables you to relish your retirement with the peace of mind that you're ready for any financial hurdles that may arise in the future. By spreading your investments across different opportunities and keeping an emergency fund in place while staying updated about economic patterns and tactics, you empower yourself with the resources to handle your finances with assurance and security. You guarantee that your golden years are filled with fulfillment and tranquility as much as possible.

4.5 EMERGENCY PLANNING: BEING PREPARED FOR THE UNEXPECTED

"We weren't prepared for the severity of the storm," exclaimed a North Carolina resident interviewed by NBC News in the aftermath of Hurricane Helene in September 2024. As you've undoubtedly experienced, life throws curveballs that can shake the foundation of your routine and peace. It's not just about the inevitable storms or power outages; emergencies encompass a broad spectrum of unexpected situations, from natural disasters to sudden health crises. Being prepared can significantly mitigate the stress and potential disruption caused by such events. Crafting a comprehensive emergency plan tailored to your specific needs and circumstances isn't just prudent; it's a fundamental aspect of safeguarding your well-being and that of your loved ones as you enjoy your retirement years.

> *Quick Tip: My parents, who lived just north of Houston, were stranded for one week, along with my sister and her husband, when Hurricane Harvey flooded the only entry/exit to their subdivision. All were thankful they had enough food on hand to support four people.*

Creating an Emergency Plan

Constructing an effective emergency plan starts with the basics: compiling a list of essential contacts, which should include family members, close friends, healthcare providers, and local emergency services. This list should be accessible—consider having physical copies in prominent places such as on your refrigerator door and near your phone, as well as digital copies saved on your mobile devices. Next, if applicable, gather and document pertinent medical information for yourself and your partner. This information should include details about medical conditions, medications, dosages, and allergies, which can be crucial in a medical emergency.

Mapping out evacuation routes and designated meeting points outside your home can enhance your preparedness, primarily if you reside in areas prone to natural disasters like hurricanes or wildfires. Familiarize yourself with local emergency plans and shelters, integrating this information into your emergency plan. Additionally, if you rely on devices that require electricity, planning for power alternatives or registering for priority restoration services with your utility company can prevent complications during power outages.

Emergency Kits

An effectively stocked emergency kit acts as a lifeline during unexpected situations. For your home, essentials include water (one gallon per person per day for several days), non-perishable food, a flashlight, batteries, a first aid kit, sanitation supplies, and extra medications. Consider the needs specific to your situation—perhaps you require spare glasses or hearing aid batteries. Clothing and blankets are also necessary, especially if you live in a colder climate, or a box fan if you live in a warm environment.

> *Quick Tip: You can never go wrong during uncertain times by maintaining a small supply of canned vegetables, fruit, juice, tuna, sardines, etc., along with a good manual can opener.*

Remember to prepare your car with an emergency kit that includes jumper cables, flares or an emergency beacon, ice scrapers, a flashlight, and a blanket. Keeping bottled water and non-perishable snacks in your vehicle can also be a lifesaver if you are stranded or must evacuate immediately.

Communication Strategies

In today's connected world, staying informed is easier but can be overwhelming. Choose a few reliable sources of information, such as local government alerts or trusted news outlets, and learn how to receive emergency notifications (e.g., via apps or text alerts). Establishing a family communication plan is important; decide how to contact one another and reconnect if separated. Ensure everyone knows how to use text messaging or mobile data services, which can be more reliable than voice calls during emergencies where network services are overloaded.

Regular Review and Practice

Like any safety or health routine, the effectiveness of your emergency plan hinges on familiarity and rehearsal. Make it a habit to review and update your plan annually, considering any changes in your medical needs, living situation, or local environment. Check supplies in your emergency kits every six months, replacing expired items as needed.

Practicing evacuation routes, testing communication plans, and conducting regular drills can significantly affect your response during an emergency. These rehearsals help refine your strategy and ensure everyone knows what to do, reducing panic and confusion at times when every second counts.

Quick Tip: As a military planning professional experienced in responding to disasters, I recall the adage from a famous General who said, "Plans are nothing, but planning is everything." It's the act of walking through this process that is most useful for those involved.

By embracing these strategies, you enhance your safety and readiness and instill a greater sense of security and confidence in your daily living. Preparedness isn't about expecting the worst; it's about ensuring peace of mind, knowing you are equipped to handle whatever comes your way, and allowing you to focus more on enjoying your well-earned retirement.

4.6 MINDFULNESS AND MEDITATION FOR A PEACEFUL RETIREMENT

In a world that often values constant activity and productivity, mindfulness and meditation practices offer a profound counterpoint, especially valuable in your retirement years. These practices are not about doing more but about being present and engaged in whatever you do, whether enjoying a quiet morning, spending time with family, or engaging in your favorite hobbies. Mindfulness and meditation can significantly reduce stress, enhance your emotional reactions to daily events, and boost your overall well-being, making your retirement more peaceful and enjoyable.

The benefits of mindfulness (active, open attention to the present) are manifold. This practice helps you become more aware of your thoughts and feelings without becoming entangled. Regularly practicing mindfulness can reduce chronic stress and boost your mood, enhance your cognitive functions by increasing your concentration and attention, and even improve your physical health by lowering blood pressure and strengthening your immune system. Meditation, a specific technique to achieve mindfulness, involves sitting quietly and paying attention to thoughts, sounds, breathing sensations, or body parts. It cultivates a state of calm and centeredness that can help you cope with the uncertainties and changes that often come with aging.

For those new to these practices, starting simple can help you integrate these techniques into your life without feeling overwhelmed. One basic exercise is focused breathing, where you sit quietly and concentrate on your breath—its rhythm, sound, and the sensation of air filling and leaving your lungs. This practice can help anchor you in the present moment, providing a quick way to return to calm when you feel stressed or anxious. Another beginner technique is the body scan, where you mentally traverse through different parts of your body, paying attention to sensations, discomfort, or relaxation. This can increase bodily awareness and highlight areas where you hold stress, guiding you in learning to relax them consciously.

Incorporating mindfulness into everyday activities can transform routine actions into moments of mindfulness that cumulatively enhance your well-being. Mindful eating, for example, involves paying full attention to the eating experience—observing your food's colors, textures, flavors and smells and the sensations of eating. This makes meals more enjoyable and can help with digestion and prevent overeating. Similarly, mindful walking—fully aware of the experience of walking, feeling the ground beneath your feet, the rhythm of your steps, and the sensations in your body—can turn a simple walk into a rejuvenating practice that clears your mind and exercises your body.

Quick Tip: I enjoy the mindfulness of my hot tub early in the pre-dawn when I can feel the warm water bubbling against my skin, watch the stars in the sky, listen as the deer meander by in the adjacent green zone, and smell the scents of nearby crape myrtle trees.

Numerous resources are available to deepen your mindfulness and meditation practices over time. Books like *Wherever You Go, There You Are* by Jon Kabat-Zinn and *The Miracle of Mindfulness* by Thich Nhat Hanh offer profound insights and practical advice on incorporating mindfulness into daily life. Apps like Headspace and Calm provide guided meditations, sleep stories, and mindfulness exercises that can be conveniently accessed from your smartphone. For a more immersive experience, consider attending a meditation retreat, which offers dedicated time and space to deepen your practice under the guidance of experienced instructors. These resources guide and structure your practice and connect you to a broader community of mindfulness practitioners, offering support and inspiration as you explore these life-enhancing practices.

By embracing mindfulness and meditation, you open yourself to a retirement filled with greater peace, enhanced awareness, and deeper enjoyment of the everyday moments that make life rich and fulfilling. These practices offer a powerful tool to navigate the complexities of life with grace and presence, ensuring your retirement years are lived with a calm and joyful heart.

4.7 THE ROLE OF PETS IN ENHANCING EMOTIONAL HEALTH

The soft purring of a cat or the joyful wagging of a dog's tail can do more than warm your heart—it can enhance your emotional and physical well-being, especially in your golden years. Pets often become companions that fill your home with joy and comfort, bringing a new sense of purpose to daily life. They're not just animals; they are friends who offer unconditional love and acceptance, making the challenges of aging a bit easier to handle. For many retirees, pets provide a type of companionship that is profoundly comforting and emotionally enriching.

> *Quick Tip: My wife bought me a dog as a retirement gift, and that miniature dachshund is fantastic. Sure, sometimes we want to travel and go out of town, which requires some coordination for boarding, but that is minor compared to the joy the dog brings our family daily.*

The emotional benefits of pet ownership are well-documented. Studies have shown that interacting with pets can significantly reduce stress levels and lower blood pressure. Caring for a pet—feeding, grooming, playing—provides structure to your day, which can be exceptionally comforting if your routine has changed significantly since retiring. Pets also encourage physical activity; walking a dog, for example, is a great way to stay active and engage with your community. This interaction helps maintain your physical health and stimulates social interactions, which are essential for your mental well-being. Moreover, the responsibility of pet care can boost your self-esteem, as successfully caring for another being is a constant reminder of your capabilities and worth.

However, deciding to bring a pet into your home during retirement requires careful consideration. Consider how a pet will fit into your lifestyle and whether you have the physical and financial resources to meet their needs. Consider the type of pet that would best match your current activity level and living situation. Dogs, for example, often require more energy and time due to their need for regular walks and social interaction. Conversely, cats might be a better option if you are looking for a less demanding companion. Birds or fish might be alternatives that bring life and companionship into your home without the need for walks or intensive care.

Financial implications are also important to consider. Pets require not just love but money. Costs include veterinary care, food, supplies, and possibly pet insurance. Unexpected health issues can also lead to significant expenses. It's wise to realistically assess whether you can handle these costs without compromising your financial security.

> *Quick Tip: I signed up for preventative dog care at our nearby PetSmart for a monthly charge, which does not cover emergencies. Since our dog is turning five, I'm weighing whether I should get a more comprehensive package. Both options are costly.*

For those who find that owning a pet is not feasible, many ways exist to enjoy the benefits of animal companionship. Volunteering at an animal shelter can be a rewarding alternative, providing opportunities to interact with pets without the long-term commitment or financial responsibility. Many shelters welcome volunteers to help with feeding, cleaning, or simply spending time playing with and caring for the animals. Another option could be visiting petting zoos or participating in community programs that bring therapy animals to facilities like libraries or senior centers. These activities can provide the joy of animal interaction and are often free or low-cost.

Quick Tip: My dad loves dogs and has had several of them throughout the years. But now, at 85, it's not practical for him to have a pet anymore. Instead, he lives close to my sister, who has two dogs, and he visits them regularly to get his needed pet exposure.

The stories of retirees finding joy and purpose through their pets are heartwarming and inspiring. Take, for example, Linda, a widow who adopted a senior dog from a local shelter. The companionship of her new friend helped alleviate her loneliness after her husband's passing and introduced her to a community of pet owners in her neighborhood. Through daily walks, she met other retirees who shared her interests, and soon, her social circle expanded, filled with new friends and fellow dog lovers. Then there's Bob, who started volunteering at a cat rescue center after retiring. He found immense satisfaction in caring for the cats and eventually adopted two, who quickly became beloved companions, filling his days with amusement and comfort.

These stories underscore the transformative impact pets can have on retirees' lives, providing companionship and a renewed sense of purpose and connection. Whether through ownership or other forms of interaction, engaging with animals can significantly improve your emotional health, enriching your retirement years with joy, comfort, and love.

4.8 STAYING SOCIALLY CONNECTED: BUILDING NEW NETWORKS

The fabric of our lives is woven with the threads of relationships, and as you step into retirement, maintaining and expanding your social network is more than just a leisure activity—it's a vital component of your well-being. Studies have consistently shown that strong social connections can lead to longer, healthier lives, significantly impacting mental and physical health. Recent research has shown that for older people, loneliness is twice as unhealthy as obesity, and chronic loneliness increases a person's chances of death by 26 percent in any given year.[7] Relationships can boost your mood, reduce the risk of mental health issues like depression and anxiety, and even promote longevity. When many social structures from your working life fall away during retirement, proactively building new networks is crucial for maintaining the quality of life you cherish.

Expanding your social circle after retirement might seem daunting, but it opens up a new realm of possibilities for forming meaningful relationships and experiences. One practical step is joining clubs or groups that align with your interests. Whether it's a book club, gardening group, or a golf league, these are places where you can meet people who share similar passions. Local community centers and libraries often host various events and workshops that allow you to learn new skills and provide a platform to connect with fellow retirees. Consider classes outside your usual comfort zone—pottery, photography, or dance. Engaging in these new activities can be incredibly rewarding and can introduce you to diverse groups of people.

Online communities also offer a vast network of connections, accessible from the comfort of your home. Platforms like Facebook, Meetup, or even forums dedicated to specific hobbies or interests can help you connect with individuals worldwide who share your enthusiasm for certain activities or subjects. These digital spaces

---

7. Waldinger, R., & Schulz, M. (2023). *The good life*. New York, NY: Simon & Schuster.

can be particularly empowering if mobility or health issues make it challenging to attend in-person events. They provide a space to share stories, exchange advice, and continue learning, keeping your mind active and engaged.

Volunteering is another enriching way to expand your social networks while giving back to the community. Whether helping out at a local food bank, mentoring young students, or working at a community garden, volunteering can connect you with people from various backgrounds, fostering a sense of purpose and belonging. These activities not only help build your social network but also instill a deep sense of satisfaction and self-worth as you contribute to the welfare of others.

Leveraging technology is indispensable in today's connected world, especially for staying in touch with family and friends who might not be nearby. Familiarize yourself with social media platforms, which can help you keep up with the lives of your loved ones and share your adventures and milestones. Video call applications like Skype, Zoom, or Google Meet can diminish the miles between you and your family, allowing for face-to-face interactions no matter where you are. These tools are invaluable for maintaining solid bonds, celebrating special occasions, and preserving those everyday moments that form the tapestry of your relationships.

Moreover, messaging apps such as WhatsApp or Telegram offer instant communication options that keep you in the loop with friends and family. They can be handy for coordinating meetups, sharing news, and staying connected throughout the day. Many of these apps also feature group chat options, making it easier to stay connected with multiple people at once, ensuring you remain a part of your loved ones' lives meaningfully.

The journey of building and maintaining new social connections in retirement is both challenging and rewarding. It requires stepping out of your comfort zone, embracing new technologies, and committing to active participation in community activities. Yet, the benefits of these efforts are profound, offering not just companionship but also enhancing your overall quality of life. As you continue to weave new threads into your social fabric, you enrich your days with shared experiences and collective wisdom, ensuring that your retirement years are vibrant, fulfilling, and joyously connected.

4.9 COPING WITH IDENTITY LOSS AFTER RETIREMENT

Retirement, a significant transition many look forward to, can also usher in an unexpected sense of loss, often related to one's identity. For decades, your profession might have offered a clear sense of who you were and how you contributed to the world. The routine, the accolades, the daily interactions, and the challenges overcome—these shaped a professional identity that suddenly shifts upon retirement. Recognizing this shift is crucial, not just as a loss, but as an opportunity to explore and redefine who you are beyond your professional life.

The first step in coping with this identity shift is acknowledging the feelings that come with it. It's okay to feel disoriented, sad, or even a bit lost without the familiar structure and purpose your job provides. These feelings are a natural part of the transition, not indicators of failing at being retired. Once you acknowledge these feelings, you can begin to redefine your identity. Reflect on aspects of your personality that were overshadowed by your career. You may possess artistic skills set aside for professional demands or a passion for gardening that can now take center stage. Retirement isn't just an end to work; it's a canvas for rediscovering and cultivating underexplored parts of yourself.

Engaging in self-discovery activities can significantly aid this transition. Journaling, for example, is more than just writing down thoughts. It is a powerful tool for introspection and can help you articulate and understand your feelings about retirement and identity. Through writing, you might discover latent interests or reaffirm values you want to prioritize in this new chapter. Attending workshops or classes can also spark new interests or rekindle old ones. These settings provide learning opportunities and can connect you with people who share similar interests, which can be incredibly affirming and supportive.

Seeking coaching is another avenue to explore. A life coach specialized in transitions can offer guidance and tools to help you navigate this new phase. They can facilitate your exploration of new roles and identities, helping you set goals that align with your redefined sense of self. This guidance can be instrumental in transforming what feels like an identity loss into an identity evolution filled with possibilities and new directions.

The stories of those who have navigated similar transitions can also be incredibly inspiring. Consider Rachel, who retired from her role as a school principal—a job that had defined her for over 30 years. She felt a significant loss of purpose and struggled with her identity after retirement. However, through volunteering at a local community center, she discovered a passion for community service that tapped into her leadership skills and desire to make a difference. Her story illustrates how the skills and attributes honed in one's career can find new expressions in retirement, contributing to a redefined, fulfilling identity.

Then there's Michael, a former corporate lawyer who has always been interested in history but has yet to have the time to pursue it. Upon retiring, he attended history classes at his local university and eventually began leading tours at historical sites. This engagement satisfied his intellectual curiosity and placed him in a new community of history enthusiasts, providing social connections that bolstered his new identity.

These stories underscore that retirement, while certainly a significant adjustment, is also a stage of life rich with opportunities to redefine and enrich your sense of self. It's about closing one chapter and having the freedom and time to start a new one—authored entirely by you, reflecting all the facets of your personality beyond just the professional. Embracing this phase with openness to change and a willingness to explore can transform the initial sense of loss into an exciting journey of self-discovery and personal growth.

4.10 THE IMPACT OF RETIREMENT ON RELATIONSHIPS AND MARRIAGE

Retirement heralds a definite shift in your daily routines and the dynamics of your closest relationships, particularly if you have a partner. The newfound time together can be a fantastic opportunity to strengthen bonds. Still, it can highlight differences that could have been less apparent when busy work schedules kept you apart. Navigating this transition alongside your partner involves understanding and adjusting to each other's evolving needs and finding ways to support one another's personal growth during this significant life change.

Navigating the transition with a partner can sometimes feel like learning to dance together on a new stage. You and your partner may discover aspects of each other's personalities that were less visible during the working years. For instance, one of you may want to dive into a host of new activities, while the other might prefer a quieter, more routine-based lifestyle. These differences don't have to be divisive. They can be an opportunity to explore new dimensions of your relationship, learning how to balance the desire to respect both partners' needs for fulfillment and independence. Approach these situations openly and flexibly, ready to negotiate and compromise while appreciating each partner's unique traits.

Effective communication is the cornerstone of navigating retirement together. It's essential to have open, honest conversations about each other's expectations for this phase of life. This might involve discussing how you envision your daily lives, your thoughts on travel and hobbies, or even your preferences for social engagements. Techniques like active and reflective listening can be helpful when you genuinely focus on understanding your partner's perspective without immediately formulating a response. Regular check-ins can also be beneficial. Schedule a dedicated time to discuss what's working well and what might need adjustment. These conversations can help prevent misunderstandings and ensure both partners feel heard and valued as they move forward.

Planning activities you can enjoy together is vital, but supporting each other's interests that might be pursued independently is equally important. For example, while one of you might enjoy golf, the other might find joy in a painting class. Spending time apart in individual pursuits can balance your relationship, giving both partners space to grow and bring new experiences into their shared lives. This not only enriches your own life but also brings added depth to the conversations and interactions you have with each other. Planning joint activities, whether a regular date night, a shared hobby, or a travel adventure, can also help maintain a connection and shared joy in your lives together.

However, couples may need help to resolve specific issues even with the best intentions. This is where relationship counseling can be a valuable tool. Seeking counseling isn't admitting failure but a proactive step toward strengthening your partnership. A counselor can provide a neutral ground for discussions, helping you explore underlying issues and develop strategies to address them constructively. Whether it's adjusting to the retirement lifestyle, reshaping your identity as a couple, or dealing with conflicts that arise, counseling can provide the tools and insights needed to navigate these challenges effectively.

Navigating retirement with your partner offers a unique opportunity to deepen your relationship, explore new horizons, and support each other's journeys. By embracing open communication, balancing joint and individual activities, and seeking support when needed, you can build a fulfilling partnership that not only withstands the challenges of this life transition but also becomes more prosperous and rewarding.

In this chapter, we explored the intricacies of building resilience in various aspects of life as you navigate the later years. From strengthening emotional and physical resilience to safeguarding financial stability and nurturing relationships, each facet is interconnected, contributing to a holistic approach to a fulfilling retirement. As we turn the page, we delve deeper into securing your financial foundation, preparing you to enjoy this enriching phase of life with peace of mind and stability.

STRATEGY 5 –
FINANCIAL SECURITY

LAYING THE FOUNDATION FOR WORRY-FREE LIVING

"Money has never made man happy, nor will it." [1]

BEN FRANKLIN

Imagine you're setting off on a long-awaited ocean voyage. The sea is vast, the possibilities endless. Think of your financial planning in the same light—a journey across an expansive ocean. The voyage could be risky without a sturdy, appropriate boat, but with the proper preparations, it becomes an adventure. This chapter is about constructing that sturdy boat, ensuring your finances are as secure and resilient as needed to carry you comfortably through retirement. According to a recent study, most Americans believe they will need $1.46 Million to retire comfortably.[2] Yet, according to a recent Federal Reserve survey, 81% of

1. Waldinger, R., & Schulz, M. (2023). *The good life*. New York, NY: Simon & Schuster.
2. Moneywise. (n.d.). Americans believe they'll need $1.46M to retire comfortably, but here's what they actually have in savings. Retrieved from https://money wise.com/retirement/retirement/americans-believe-theyll-need-146m-to-retire-

retirees who only had $50,000 to $100,000 in savings are doing OK or living comfortably.[3] That's because many retirees have other income sources. For example, in 2023, 80% of retirees aged 65-plus reported one or more private income sources, such as a pension, employment or interest, dividends, or rental income.[4] As we discussed earlier, money is usually not the answer to happiness. But this chapter will focus on securing your financial future and identifying funds for your retirement priorities.

5.1 CREATING A BULLETPROOF RETIREMENT BUDGET

Establishing a Realistic Budget

Creating a budget for your retirement might seem daunting at first —it's about predicting your future needs and aligning them with what you've saved over many years of hard work. However, budgeting puts you in control and empowers you to make informed decisions. Think of this process as crafting a detailed map that will guide you through the financial aspects of retirement. Start by listing all your predictable income sources—Social Security, pensions, annuities, and any passive income streams. Then, outline your fixed and variable expenses. Fixed expenses might include housing, utilities, food, and insurance, while variable costs could encompass travel, entertainment, restaurants, and hobbies. This cash flow exercise is depicted below in Figure 4. It is all about money coming in and going out of your household. This

---

comfortably-but-heres-what-they-actually-have-in-savings?utm_source=syn_apple news_mon&utm_medium=Z&utm_campaign=60599&utm_content= syn_ob6c3454-c373-449a-ab33-675a542492cd , accessed on 7/24/24.

3. https://apple.news/AXvsfE_gZT-G7QJmr3ZnoKg , accessed on 8/15/24.

4. https://apple.news/AXvsfE_gZT-G7QJmr3ZnoKg , accessed on 8/15/24.

initial mapping will give you a clear picture of your financial land-scape, helping you navigate retirement without unnecessary financial stress.

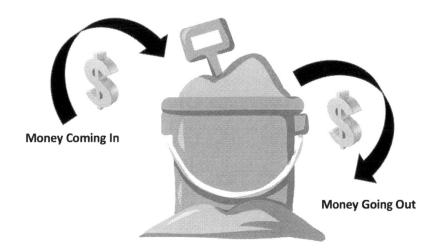

Money Coming In

Money Going Out

Figure 4. Household Cash Flow

Quick Tip: In the bonus Chapter 6 at the end of this book, I've provided a link to free budget tools you can download.

Prioritizing Expenses

Once you have a clear view of your income and expenditures, the next step is to prioritize your expenses. You cannot avoid essential expenses—housing, food, healthcare, and insurance premiums. Discretionary expenses, however, are areas where you can exercise some control. These might include leisure travel, hobbies, or dining out. Adjusting your spending priorities might not always be easy, especially if it involves cutting back on activities you enjoy, but it can significantly enhance your financial stability. Think of this prioritization as strategically deciding where to allocate your resources to maximize your happiness and security. Now is the time to reflect on your ikigai and your bucket list to understand what is most important to fund.

Adjusting for Inflation

Inflation is an often underestimated factor that can erode your purchasing power over time. It's the gradual increase in prices and the corresponding decrease in the value of money. That's why 89% of recent survey respondents named inflation their top concern.[5] When planning your retirement budget, it's crucial to account for inflation—especially considering that healthcare costs, which will likely make up a significant portion of your expenses, tend to rise faster than general inflation. To guard against this, consider inflation-protected income sources like TIPS (Treasury Inflation-Protected Securities) or increasing annuities that offer some protection against rising costs. Social Security adjusts for inflation annually, as do federal government pensions. Adjusting your budget annually to reflect changes in inflation rates can help maintain your purchasing power throughout retirement.

Utilizing Budgeting Tools

In today's digital age, numerous tools and apps can help you manage your retirement budget effectively. These tools often offer expense tracking, budget alerts, and investment monitoring. For instance, apps like Mint (now transitioned to Credit Karma) or PocketGuard link to your bank accounts and automatically categorize your spending. This makes it easier to stick to your budget and

---

5. https://www.cnbc.com/2024/05/09/4percent-of-current-retirees-say-they-are-living-the-dream-survey-finds.html , accessed on 9/19/24.

spot areas where you need more money. Utilizing these tools can take much of the guesswork and manual tracking out of budget management, allowing you to focus more on enjoying your retirement.

> *Quick Tip: In the bonus Chapter 6, I also provide a link for 30 days of free access to MFPA Vault, my secure client service that leverages the RightCapital platform used by CFP® Professionals. This bank-level security platform is excellent for planning and tracking your retirement for less than $1 per day, and it puts you totally in control.*

By taking these steps—establishing a realistic budget, prioritizing expenses, adjusting for inflation, and utilizing budgeting tools—you set the stage for a financially stable retirement. It's about having the freedom to enjoy your achievements without the burden of financial stress, ensuring that your retirement years are indeed the best of your life.

5.2 DOWNSIZING FOR FINANCIAL AND EMOTIONAL FREEDOM

Imagine the home where you've celebrated milestones, raised children, and created countless memories. Now, as you approach or navigate retirement, you may consider the possibility of downsizing—transitioning to a smaller space that promises financial relief and a newfound freedom in your golden years. Downsizing isn't merely about moving to a smaller residence; it's about reshaping your environment to better suit your current lifestyle and aspirations. This move can significantly reduce your daily responsibilities and financial burdens, allowing you to allocate more resources—both time and money—toward enjoying your retirement.

Benefits of Downsizing

The financial benefits of downsizing are often the most tangible. Moving to a smaller home can reduce or eliminate a mortgage payment if you buy the new home outright. This shift can also free up substantial funds previously tied to housing expenses. Additionally, smaller homes typically incur lower property taxes, reduced utility costs, and less money spent on maintenance and repairs. However, the advantages extend beyond the financial. Emotionally, downsizing can signify a new chapter, one less burdened by the upkeep of a larger property and more focused on new experiences. It can also bring relief, simplifying your lifestyle and reducing the stress of managing a larger property. This newfound simplicity can lead to a more explicit focus on what truly brings joy and fulfillment.

Steps to Downsize

The process of downsizing requires careful planning and consideration. Begin by assessing your current possessions. What items are essential? What can be donated, sold, or discarded? This step often involves significant emotional decisions, particularly when parting with sentimental items. However, it's also an opportunity to declutter and simplify your life, focusing on what you truly need and cherish. Next, consider what type of new residence will suit your lifestyle. Do you crave a bustling community or prefer solitude and quiet? Would a condo offer the convenience and community you desire, or is a small, manageable house more appealing? Once you've defined your ideal living situation, research and visit potential homes and neighborhoods. Consider factors such as accessibility, proximity to family or friends, and available services and amenities that match your lifestyle and health needs.

> *Quick Tip: Consider what location best meets your needs, not the needs of your children or grandchildren. My wife and I visit our grandkids all over the USA, so any location is fair game for us because we have to travel to see others regardless of where we live.*

Financial Implications

From a financial perspective, downsizing can lead to significant savings, which can be redirected toward securing a more comfortable and enjoyable retirement. Reduced utility bills, lower property taxes, and minimal maintenance are just a few areas where you can save. Furthermore, downsizing enables you to liquidate equity from a larger home. In that case, these funds can be reinvested into savings or used to cover living expenses, travel, or leisure activities that enhance your quality of life. It's best to work with a financial advisor to understand the full implications of selling your home and moving to a smaller property, ensuring the decision aligns with your overall financial goals and retirement plan. Remember, If you have a capital gain from the sale of your main home, you may qualify to exclude up to $250,000 of that gain from your income or up to $500,000 if you file a joint return with your spouse.[6]

---

6. https://www.irs.gov/taxtopics/tc701 , accessed on 8/06/24.

Emotional Considerations

While the benefits of downsizing are clear, the emotional impact of leaving a long-term home can be profound. Your home likely holds countless memories and signifies significant chapters in your life. The thought of leaving can evoke feelings of sadness and loss. Acknowledging and recognizing these feelings as a natural part of the process is important. Engage with family and friends, share your thoughts and concerns, and allow yourself to grieve the change. However, also try to focus on the positive aspects of downsizing—the opportunity to create new memories, the reduction of daily burdens, and the ability to live more freely. Many find that once they've settled into their new home, they feel rejuvenated and excited by the possibilities.

In embracing downsizing, you're not just choosing a smaller living space; you're opting for a lifestyle that can lead to greater financial freedom and emotional well-being. This transition, while significant, opens up a spectrum of opportunities to redefine your retirement, making it as fulfilling and enjoyable as possible.

5.3 MANAGING DEBT BEFORE AND DURING RETIREMENT

Strategies to Eliminate Debt

As you approach retirement, the specter of debt can loom large, casting a shadow over what should be a time of relaxation and enjoyment. The good news is that with thoughtful planning and disciplined action, you can reduce or even eliminate your debt before you retire. Refinancing your existing loans can be a powerful strategy, especially in an environment of historically low interest rates. By refinancing your mortgage, for instance, you may secure a lower interest rate, which can significantly reduce your monthly payments and total interest cost over the life of the loan. Debt consolidation is another effective tool, particularly if juggling multiple credit card balances or other high-interest debts. Combining these into a single, lower-interest loan can simplify your finances and reduce the amount of interest you pay, making it easier to pay down your debt faster.

Considering these options, consulting with a financial advisor who understands your financial situation and can guide you toward decisions supporting your long-term financial health is essential. They can help you assess the benefits and drawbacks of refinancing or consolidating your debt, considering closing costs, loan terms, and your expected retirement timeline. Remember, the goal is to reduce debt and optimize your financial situation to support a stress-free retirement.

Managing Mortgage Debt

Whether to pay off your mortgage before you retire is a significant decision that depends on your financial situation and the emotional comfort of being mortgage-free. For many, entering retirement without a mortgage can provide tremendous financial relief and stability. However, weighing this against the potential benefits of maintaining your mortgage is necessary, such as preserving cash for other investments that might offer higher returns or maintaining liquidity for unexpected expenses.

If you choose to keep your mortgage into retirement, consider whether the terms align with your current financial goals and retirement plan. It might make sense to refinance to a lower rate or a type of mortgage that offers more flexibility or lower monthly payments. Suppose you're close to paying off your mortgage. In that case, it might be beneficial to accelerate your payments to eliminate the debt faster, reducing your monthly expenses and interest burden in retirement.

Credit Card and Consumer Debt

High-interest debt, particularly from credit cards, can be one of the most pernicious obstacles to financial freedom in retirement. Tackling this type of debt requires a focused strategy. Start by making a complete list of your debts, along with their interest rates and balances. Prioritize paying off the debts with the highest interest rates first while maintaining minimum payments on others. This strategy, often called the avalanche method, saves you the most money in interest over time.

Another effective method is the snowball method, where you pay off the smallest debts first, gaining momentum as each balance is cleared. This can be particularly motivating as you see the decrease in debt. Additionally, consider transferring high-interest credit card balances to a card with a 0% introductory rate on balance transfers. This allows you to pay the balance without accruing interest, but be mindful of any transfer fees (often 3% or more) and the rate after the introductory period ends.

Impact of Debt on Retirement Plans

Carrying significant debt into retirement can severely impact your financial security and lifestyle. Monthly debt payments can eat into your retirement income, reducing the funds available for everyday expenses, healthcare, and leisure activities. Moreover, unexpected costs or financial shocks, such as medical emergencies, can be more challenging to manage without the cushion of an emergency savings fund.

The psychological impact of debt can also be considerable. Worrying about debt can lead to stress, affecting your health and well-being. Achieving a debt-free status as you enter retirement can lift a mental burden, allowing you to enjoy your retirement years with peace of mind fully.

Managing debt effectively as you approach retirement is not just about improving your financial situation—it's about setting the stage for a delightful and fulfilling retirement. By focusing on eliminating high-interest debts, considering the appropriate strategy for your mortgage, and using tools like refinancing and consolidation wisely, you can secure your financial foundation and look forward to a retirement characterized by freedom and stability rather than uncertainty and stress.

5.4 DECODING RETIREMENT ACCOUNTS: 401(K)S AND IRAS SIMPLIFIED

Navigating the landscape of retirement accounts can feel like deciphering a complex map with numerous paths and directions. Let's simplify this journey together, focusing on the most common types of accounts: 401(k)s and Individual Retirement Accounts (IRAs). Understanding the fundamental differences and benefits of each can significantly influence how you plan and secure your financial future.

A 401(k) plan, often offered through employers, allows you to save a portion of your pre-tax salary. The taxes on these earnings are deferred until you withdraw the funds, typically during retirement when your income may be lower, potentially leading to a lower tax rate on the withdrawals. On the other hand, IRAs come in two main types: Traditional and Roth. Traditional IRAs are similar to 401(k)s in terms of tax treatment, where contributions may be tax-deductible, and taxes on earnings are deferred until withdrawal. Roth IRAs, however, are funded with after-tax dollars, meaning the contributions are not tax-deductible, but the withdrawals, including earnings, are tax-free in retirement.

The choice between these accounts often depends on your current and expected future tax situations or Required Minimum Distributions (RMDs). Suppose you anticipate being in a higher tax bracket in retirement or believe that tax rates will rise. In that case, a Roth IRA is more beneficial as it locks in your tax liabilities at lower rates. Furthermore, Roth IRAs have no required minimum distributions ever. Conversely, if you expect to be in a lower tax bracket in retirement, a Traditional IRA or a 401(k) is more advantageous, allowing you to defer taxes until you withdraw the funds at a lower rate. However, a traditional IRA will now require minimum distributions beginning at age 73.[7]

Contribution Limits and Timing

Understanding the nuances of contribution limits and the timing of your contributions can also play a pivotal role in maximizing the benefits of these retirement accounts. For 2024, individuals with earned income can contribute up to $23,000 to a 401(k) plan, with a catch-up contribution of an additional $7,000 for those aged 50 and over ($30,000 total). Similarly, the earned income contribution limit for Traditional and Roth IRAs is $7,000, with a catch-up limit of an additional $1,000 for those 50 and older ($8,000 total).

---

7. https://www.irs.gov/retirement-plans/plan-participant-employee/retirement-topics-required-minimum-distributions-rmds , accessed on 8/06/24.

Making these contributions as early in the year as possible can significantly enhance your investment returns over time due to the potential for longer interest compounding.

> *Quick Tip: I had a client who asked if he could contribute to an IRA using only his Social Security income. I wondered if he had any other 'earned income' from a W2 form, and he said no. I advised him he could not contribute to an IRA since he had no 'earned income.' Social Security income is not 'earned income' by the IRS definition. The same holds for VA Disability income and Federal government pensions. None generate a W2 for 'earned income.'*

Moreover, if you are nearing the end of the year and still need to maximize your contributions, consider increasing your retirement savings in those final months. This will reduce your annual taxable income while increasing your retirement savings. It's a strategic move that benefits your present and future financial states.

The Rollover Process

Perhaps you've changed jobs over the years and accumulated multiple 401(k) plans with different employers. Consolidating these into a single IRA can simplify financial management and reduce administrative fees. The process, known as a rollover, involves moving funds from your 401(k) into an IRA. It can be done without incurring immediate tax penalties if completed within 60 days. A direct rollover, where funds are transferred directly between financial institutions, is a seamless method that avoids the mandatory withholding of funds typical of an indirect rollover.

Consolidation simplifies your financial landscape and provides a broader range of investment options than you'd have in employer-sponsored 401(k) plans. With more choices, you can tailor your investment strategies more closely to your personal risk tolerance and retirement goals.

Addressing Common Misconceptions

Finally, let's clear up some common misconceptions. A prevalent myth is that you cannot contribute to an IRA if you contribute to a 401(k). This is not true; you can contribute to both. However, the deductibility of your IRA contributions may be limited based on your income and whether you or your spouse has access to a workplace retirement plan. Understanding these nuances is crucial in maximizing the potential of your retirement savings.

Another common misunderstanding is that IRAs are only for the self-employed or those without a 401(k). In reality, anyone with earned income can contribute to an IRA, making it a versatile tool for retirement savings, regardless of your employment situation.

By demystifying these aspects of retirement accounts, you can make informed decisions that bolster your financial security. This will ensure that when the time comes, you can retire with peace of mind, knowing your finances are well-arranged and your future is secure.

5.5 SMART INVESTMENT STRATEGIES FOR THOSE 50+

As we mature into our golden years, our investment approach must evolve to reflect our changing priorities and risk tolerance. Understanding and implementing innovative investment strategies is crucial, not just to preserve what we have worked so hard to accumulate but also to ensure it continues to grow and provide for our needs throughout retirement. Managing investment risks effectively becomes paramount, as the consequences of significant losses are more pronounced when time is no longer on your side, and you are no longer in the workforce generating a steady income.

Risk Management in Investments

Think of your investment as a garden. Just as a well-maintained garden balances sun and shade, your investment portfolio needs a balanced approach to managing risk. This balance is crucial, especially if you are over 50 when the time to recover from financial setbacks significantly shortens. Remember, time is NOT on your side. Diversification is your sunblock, shielding you from the harsh impacts of volatility while ensuring you still enjoy the growth opportunities that sunny days bring. It's about having a mix of investments that react differently to the same economic event. This means spreading your investments across different asset classes like stocks, bonds, and real estate and, within those classes, diversifying across industries and geographies. This strategy helps mitigate the risk of significant losses, as it is unlikely that all sectors or regions will perform poorly simultaneously.

Moreover, consider the timing of your investments. As retirement approaches, the strategy should shift from accumulation to preservation. This shift may reduce exposure to high-volatility stocks in favor of more stable assets, such as bonds or dividend-paying stocks, which can provide regular income. This doesn't mean avoiding stocks altogether but adjusting the mix to reduce risk and stabilize investment returns.

Quick Tip: In the bonus Chapter 6, I've also included a link to a FREE risk assessment survey from the University of Missouri. The results of this quick assessment will classify you into one of five risk categories, from low-risk tolerance to high-risk tolerance. This can be helpful information for sharing with your financial advisor or registered investment professional.

Investing in Annuities

Annuities can be a compelling option when creating a steady income stream during retirement. Annuities are financial products that you purchase from an insurance company. They can provide you with a steady income for a fixed period of your lifetime, which is a significant benefit, ensuring you preserve your resources. However, the decision to invest in annuities should be approached with a complete understanding of their pros and cons. Ongoing research covering thousands of older Americans shows retirees are happier, healthier, and more satisfied when they have guaranteed monthly paychecks to cover basic needs.[8]

On the positive side, annuities provide financial stability and predictability. By providing a guaranteed income, they can complement other retirement incomes, such as Social Security. On the downside, annuities often require a significant upfront investment, and the funds you invest in an annuity can be locked in, meaning you have limited access to these funds should you need them for an unexpected expense. Moreover, the fees associated

---

8.   https://www.tiaa.org/public/plansponsors/insights/tmrw/edition-2/retirement-happiness-factors-and-annuities-benefits-b#:~:text=Accord-ing%20to%20a%20Rand%20Corporation,very%20satisfied" %20than%20those%20without. , accessed on 9/10/24.

with annuities can be high, and they can be complex financial products that might be challenging to understand fully.

Given these factors, it's necessary to carefully assess whether an annuity fits your financial situation and retirement goals. Please consult a financial advisor to make this decision and ensure you choose an annuity that best meets your needs and fully understands its terms and conditions.

Staying Informed on Market Trends

Keeping a pulse on market trends is as important as ever. Economic conditions, interest rates, and market trends can significantly impact investment returns and retirement planning. Staying informed allows you to adjust your investment strategy in response to changing economic conditions. For example, if economic indicators suggest an upcoming recession, you might consider shifting some of your investment allocations into more conservative investments to protect against significant losses.

Numerous resources are available to help you stay informed, from financial news outlets and investment podcasts to newsletters from financial experts. However, the key is consuming this information to see how it applies to your investment strategy. Always filter this information through the lens of your long-term financial goals and consult with your financial advisor to understand how certain trends might impact your specific situation.

Identifying Passive Income Options

Creating streams of passive income can significantly enhance your financial security in retirement. Passive income is money you earn without actively working for it—the "set it and forget it" of your income streams. Real estate is a popular source of passive income. Whether rental income from a property you own or earnings from a real estate investment trust (REIT), suitable real estate investments can provide consistent cash flow. An alternative option is creating and selling digital products, such as e-books or online courses, based on your professional expertise or hobbies.

Peer-to-peer lending is another avenue for lending money to individuals or small businesses online through platforms like Prosper.com that match lenders with borrowers. This type of investment can offer higher returns than traditional banks' savings accounts or CDs, although it also comes with greater risk.

When exploring passive income options, evaluating the potential returns against the risks and your capacity to manage these investments is crucial. Some passive income streams require more management and oversight, and some carry significant financial risk. As with all investments, diversifying your passive income sources can help manage risk while providing multiple income streams. The question is whether these investments fit your risk assessment profile.

By embracing these investment strategies—managing risks effectively, considering annuities, staying informed about market trends, and exploring passive income options—you can ensure that your retirement finances are robust, flexible, and capable of supporting your lifestyle and aspirations in the coming years. This approach lets you enjoy your retirement with the peace of mind that your finances are secure, leaving you free to focus on the joys of this richly deserved time.

5.6 CREATING A SUSTAINABLE WITHDRAWAL STRATEGY: THE 4% RULE

When you think about your retirement funds, it's like considering a reservoir from which you'll draw water to sustain you through many seasons. The 4% rule has long been a cornerstone in retirement planning. It is akin to a wise old gauge that helps many retirees measure how much to withdraw annually from their savings without depleting their reservoir too soon. Originating from a study by financial advisor William Bengen in 1994, the rule suggests that you can withdraw 4% of your retirement portfolio in the first year of retirement and adjust that amount each subsequent year for inflation. The beauty of this rule lies in its simplicity and starting point for planning, providing a baseline from which you can adjust based on personal needs and market conditions.

However, the economic landscape has evolved significantly since the 1990s, and so has the life expectancy of many retirees. These shifts necessitate a closer look and possibly adjustments to this rule. For instance, during prolonged market downturns, sticking rigidly to a 4% withdrawal rate might accelerate the depletion of your funds if your investments are also declining in value. Conversely, in a robust market, your investments grow well beyond your withdrawal rate, potentially allowing for a higher withdrawal rate without jeopardizing the longevity of your funds.

This nuanced understanding of the 4% rule highlights the importance of flexibility in your withdrawal strategy. Adjusting your withdrawals in response to market performance can help preserve your capital during downturns and take advantage of growth during good times. For example, reduce your withdrawal rate to 3% in a down market or delay certain discretionary expenses to help your portfolio recover. Conversely, in a thriving market, you might increase your withdrawal rate slightly or take a lump sum to cover a significant expense, such as a dream vacation or a family reunion.

The alternatives to the 4% rule are varied and cater to different types of investment portfolios and retirement lifestyles. For some, a dynamic spending approach, which adjusts withdrawals based on the portfolio's performance each year, provides a balance between maintaining lifestyle and ensuring the longevity of funds. Others might prefer a bucket strategy, which involves dividing your retirement savings into several 'buckets' earmarked for different time segments of your retirement. Each bucket can be invested differently, ranging from highly liquid assets for immediate needs to more growth-oriented investments for later years. This approach not only helps in managing sequence risk but also in addressing different expenditure needs at various stages of retirement. Sequence risk is the unfavorable order and timing of investment returns, resulting in less retirement money.

Incorporating expert opinions into your retirement planning can further refine your withdrawal strategy. Financial planners often bring a wealth of experience and can provide personalized advice based on an in-depth analysis of your financial situation, lifestyle needs, and market conditions. They can help you navigate the complexities of market volatility, tax implications, and unexpected expenses, ensuring that your withdrawal strategy is robust and flexible.

By understanding and integrating these strategies, you can tailor a withdrawal plan that starts with the 4% rule as a benchmark and adapts to the market realities and your personal needs. This approach ensures that your retirement savings provide you with a well-maintained reservoir that will support you through all the seasons of your retirement.

5.7 MAXIMIZING YOUR SOCIAL SECURITY BENEFITS

According to a recent Gallup and West Health poll, 80% of people under age 62 worry Social Security won't be available when needed. So the question becomes: When should I start taking my Social Security? Navigating the intricacies of Social Security benefits is akin to decoding a vital code that unlocks a steady income stream during your golden years. Understanding your options and the strategies to maximize these benefits can significantly impact your financial security and comfort in retirement. Social Security is a foundation upon which many Americans build their retirement plans. It's structured to provide you with a continuous income, adjusted annually for inflation, which helps ensure your basic needs are met even as the cost of living rises.

> *Quick Tip: My parents took Social Security at 62 because they needed the income. But I plan on waiting until age 70 because I don't need the income now, and I want to create a higher-value inflation-adjusted annuity for my spouse after I die. When to take Social Security is a highly personal and situational decision requiring significant thought and not based on a spur-of-the-moment decision. My advice: consult a CFP® Professional.*

Understanding Benefit Options

Social Security offers a variety of benefits, and knowing the nuances of each can help you make the most of what you've rightfully earned. The program is designed to provide retirement benefits based on your 35 highest-earning years. If you have fewer than 35 years in the workforce, zeros are averaged in, which can significantly reduce your benefits. For those who have had lower earnings in some years or took time off for family or personal reasons, it might be beneficial to work a bit longer to replace low-earning years with higher ones, thereby increasing the average and consequently the benefits. Additionally, many are unaware of some benefits, such as spousal benefits, which allow you to claim benefits based on your spouse's work record if they are higher than yours, and survivor benefits, which provide your spouse with continued benefits after your death.

Timing for Claiming Benefits

The age at which you choose to start claiming Social Security benefits dramatically impacts the monthly amount you receive. You can begin receiving benefits as early as age 62, but doing so may reduce your benefits by as much as 30% compared to waiting until your full retirement age (FRA), which varies from 66 to 67, depending on your birth year. Each year you delay claiming past your FRA up to age 70, your benefits increase by about 8% annually. This significant increase can be a game-changer in ensuring your retirement savings last, especially if you live well into your 80s or beyond. When filing for benefits, you should consider your health, financial needs, and other income sources. If you have good health and other resources, delaying benefits to maximize the payout makes sense. However, claiming earlier may be better if you need immediate income or have health concerns.

Coordinating with Spousal Benefits

For married couples, coordinating when and how you claim Social Security can optimize your combined benefits. If one spouse earned significantly more than the other, it might make sense for the higher earner to delay benefits to maximize the survivor benefit for the other spouse. This strategy ensures that the surviving spouse will continue to receive the highest possible amount (this is my strategy in the Quick Tip above). Additionally, one spouse can claim retirement benefits early while the other person delays theirs. Later, the spouse who claimed early might switch to spousal benefits if half of the other's benefit amount at FRA surpasses their own. Navigating these options can be complex, but with careful planning and perhaps guidance from a financial advisor, you can maximize your Social Security income.

Handling Social Security Taxation

Many retirees are surprised that their Social Security benefits may be subject to federal income tax. Suppose your combined income — which includes your adjusted gross income, nontaxable interest, and half of your Social Security benefits — exceeds certain thresholds. In that case, you may owe taxes on a portion of your benefits. For most, up to 50% of benefits could be taxable; for those with higher combined incomes, up to 85% could be taxed. Planning for these taxes is crucial to avoid surprises and ensure a steady net income. Strategies such as spreading out withdrawals from other retirement accounts or investing in Roth IRAs, where withdrawals are tax-free, can help manage how much your Social Security benefits are taxed. Careful planning concerning the timing and amount of withdrawals from other retirement savings can be essential in minimizing the tax impact on your Social Security benefits.

Understanding and maximizing your Social Security benefits is more than just a financial necessity; it's about ensuring you have a stable foundation to build your retirement dreams. You can optimize this valuable resource by comprehensively exploring your options, strategically timing your benefits, coordinating with your spouse, and planning for potential taxes. With these strategies in place, Social Security can provide you with financial comfort and peace of mind, allowing you to enjoy your retirement years with the security and dignity you deserve.

5.8 EFFECTIVE TAX PLANNING STRATEGIES FOR RETIREES

Navigating the complexities of tax planning as a retiree can feel akin to charting a course through uncharted waters. Each decision you make, from the types of accounts you withdraw from to the state you choose to call home, can significantly impact your tax liabilities and financial well-being in retirement. A strategic approach to managing these factors can help ensure that more of your hard-earned money stays in your pocket, supporting a more comfortable and secure retirement.

Focus on Tax-Efficient Withdrawal Strategies

One of the most effective tools in your tax planning arsenal is understanding how to withdraw from your various accounts strategically. You likely have a mix of taxable, tax-deferred, and tax-free accounts. The order in which you withdraw funds from these can significantly impact your tax bill. I am not a Certified Public Accountant (CPA), but I recommend consulting one. It might be tempting to delay tapping into your tax-deferred accounts like traditional IRAs and 401(k)s to benefit from continued tax-deferred growth. However, this could lead to higher required minimum distributions (RMDs) later, potentially pushing you into a higher tax bracket. A balanced approach often involves blending withdrawals from taxable and tax-deferred accounts each year to manage your tax bracket more effectively. Additionally, consider using tax-free withdrawals from a Roth IRA or 401(k) strategically to avoid bumping into a higher tax bracket, especially in years where you might have higher-than-usual income.

Leverage Tax Credits and Deductions for Seniors

As a retiree, you are eligible for several tax credits and deductions to reduce your liability. For instance, once you reach age 65, you qualify for a higher standard deduction. For the tax year 2024, this additional deduction is $1,550 for each married person and $1,950 for singles. This higher deduction can help lower your taxable income. Additionally, medical expenses can become substantial in retirement, and the IRS allows you to deduct qualified medical expenses that exceed 7.5% of your adjusted gross income (AGI). This can include everything from Medicare premiums to dental work, and understanding how to leverage this deduction can yield considerable tax relief.

Plan for Required Minimum Distributions (RMDs)

For most retirees, RMDs, which must start at age 73, can be a significant tax planning challenge. These mandatory withdrawals from your tax-deferred retirement accounts can push you into a higher tax bracket and increase your Medicare Part B and Part D premiums due to income-related monthly adjustment amounts

(IRMAA). Planning for these distributions involves understanding how much you need to withdraw and strategizing how to use these funds effectively. For example, if you find you don't need all the money from an RMD for living expenses, consider reinvesting the funds in a taxable account or using them for gifting to benefit from annual exclusion gifts, which can help reduce your taxable estate.

Consider the Impact of State Taxes

Your retirement location can significantly affect your tax liabilities. Some states, like Florida and Nevada, do not tax individual income, which can mean significant savings, especially if you receive substantial income from retirement accounts or Social Security. Other states offer tax incentives for retirees, such as exemptions on certain types of retirement income or property tax breaks for seniors. If you are considering relocating in retirement, compare the tax implications of potential new homes. This comparison should go beyond income taxes to assess sales, property, and estate or inheritance taxes, which can impact your financial health.

Roth Conversions

A Roth conversion involves transferring funds from a tax-deferred account, like a traditional IRA, into a Roth IRA, where future withdrawals are tax-free. This strategy can be particularly beneficial if you expect to be in a higher tax bracket in retirement or if you aim to leave tax-free money to your heirs. The converted amount is taxable in the year of the conversion, so careful timing is necessary to avoid a significant tax hit. Ideally, you want to execute conversions in years with lower income, smoothing out your tax liabilities and potentially keeping you in a lower tax bracket. Regularly assessing your financial landscape and consulting with a tax professional can help determine if and when a Roth conversion makes sense for your situation. Remember that Roth accounts are not subject to any Required Minimum Distribution (RMD) requirements.

By understanding and strategically managing these aspects of tax planning, you can maximize your financial resources in retirement. This proactive approach ensures compliance with tax laws and aligns with your financial goals, providing peace of mind and financial security in your retirement years.

5.9 PROTECTING AGAINST SENIOR FINANCIAL ABUSE

Understanding and preventing financial abuse is crucial for maintaining your independence and securing your well-being in retirement. It's a sadly common issue that often goes unrecognized, masquerading as genuine help or concern from others. Financial abuse involves the unauthorized use of an older adult's funds or property, either by a caregiver, a family member, or a stranger. Recognizing the signs of this abuse is the first step toward protection. These signs can be subtle, such as sudden changes in your bank accounts, unexplained withdrawals, or alterations to your will or other financial documents. More overt signs might include someone preventing you from accessing your funds or receiving bills for services you never received.

Quick Tip: I recommend an identity protection service as an excellent way to prevent abuse and flag it quickly for resolution. I have used LifeLock for ten years and am very happy with its service. For less than $20 per month, you get *peace of mind and $1 million in protection from identity theft.*

You should meticulously organize and protect your financial documents and accounts to shield yourself from such vulnerabilities. Keep your financial records secure, including bank statements, wills, and insurance policies, in a fire-proof vault. Only share access with individuals you trust implicitly, and maintain oversight of your accounts even then. Regularly reviewing your financial statements can help you spot unauthorized transactions quickly. Consider setting up alerts with your bank to notify you of any significant transactions or changes to your account settings. Consider locking down your credit so no one can open a new credit card account.

When it comes to legal protections, there are several avenues you can pursue if you suspect financial abuse. Every state has different laws regarding senior financial abuse, but all provide some means of recourse. Reporting the abuse to local authorities is a crucial first step. You may also need to contact your bank to freeze your accounts and prevent unauthorized access. Legal actions can include revoking a power of attorney if the person named has abused their position or suing for recovery of stolen assets. Consulting with an attorney specializing in senior law can provide guidance tailored to your situation, ensuring your rights are fully protected.

For support and resources, numerous organizations are dedicated to helping victims of senior financial abuse. The National Center on Elder Abuse (NCEA) and the Financial Industry Regulatory Authority (FINRA) offer resources and guidance on responding to financial abuse. Local senior centers and social services can also assist and direct you to community resources that can help.

Remember, seeking help is a strength, not a weakness. By staying informed and vigilant, you empower yourself to stand against financial abuse, ensuring your retirement remains secure and serene, free from exploitation.

5.10 USER-FRIENDLY FINANCIAL TOOLS FOR EVERYDAY USE

In today's digital age, embracing technology can significantly streamline managing your finances, especially during retirement when simplicity and efficiency become paramount. For many, the transition to using financial apps may seem daunting, laden with concerns about complexity and security. However, the reality is that many of these tools are designed with user-friendliness in mind, specifically catering to those who might need to be more tech-savvy. These apps can transform how you handle your finances, from daily budget tracking to overseeing long-term investments and everything in between.

The advantages of integrating technology into your financial management are manifold. Firstly, the precision of digital tools is unmatched. Human error in calculations or oversight can lead to significant discrepancies in your financial tracking. Apps automate these processes, ensuring that mistakes are minimized and your financial data remains accurate. Moreover, the convenience of having all your financial information accessible in one place at the touch of a button cannot be overstated. Whether checking your latest transactions, monitoring investment performance, or setting budget reminders, these tools can provide a comprehensive overview of your financial health and keep you from sifting through mountains of paperwork.

Furthermore, the real-time tracking capabilities of many financial apps mean you can get an instantaneous view of your financial status. This immediacy can be particularly beneficial for adjusting spending habits or making quick financial decisions. It's like having a financial advisor in your pocket, one that keeps you constantly informed and ready to act as needed.

A step-by-step guide can ease the transition for those ready to use these digital tools. Begin by choosing an app that meets your financial needs—budgeting, investment tracking, or expense reporting. Look for apps that offer a straightforward, intuitive interface and prioritize ease of use. Once selected, take the time to familiarize yourself with the app's functionalities. Most apps offer a tutorial or a help section to guide new users. Input your financial information and customize the settings to suit your preferences, such as setting up notifications for bill payments or setting financial goals.

While the benefits of using financial apps are clear, approach these tools with an awareness of privacy and security. The digital nature of these apps means that they contain sensitive personal and financial information, which can be vulnerable to security breaches if not adequately protected.

To safeguard your information, check that any financial app you use employs strong security measures such as encryption, two-factor authentication, and secure servers. Be wary of apps that request unnecessary permissions that could lead to data being shared or sold without your consent. Additionally, maintain strong, unique passwords for your financial accounts and change them regularly to prevent unauthorized access. Always download apps from reputable sources such as the Google Play Store or Apple App Store to avoid counterfeit applications that could compromise your data.

In this digital era, integrating technology into your financial management strategy offers a blend of accuracy, convenience, and control, empowering you to manage your retirement finances more effectively and securely. You can enhance and streamline your financial management practices by choosing the right tools, taking the time to learn how to use them, and prioritizing the security of your financial data.

As we wrap up this discussion on user-friendly financial tools, it's clear how helpful they are in crafting a secure and efficient financial management system. Today's digital tools can transform the mundane tasks of tracking expenses and managing budgets into a seamless, integrated part of your daily life. With these systems in place, you're better equipped to focus on enjoying your retirement, knowing that your finances are well-handled and protected.

BONUSES: EASY LINKS TO RESOURCES

"Make people an offer so good they would feel stupid saying no."

ALEX HORMOZI

I magine you've just finished a fascinating novel that leaves you with more questions than answers, urging you to dive deeper into its themes and characters. In many ways, the journey of retirement is similar—constantly evolving, filled with new chapters and unexpected twists. As you turn each page, wouldn't it be wonderful to have a guide or a companion that could offer insights, tools, and resources precisely when you need them? That's the essence of this bonus chapter: to equip you with practical, accessible resources that complement the strategies and stories we've explored together.

6.1 FREE RESILIENCE COURSE

Your Path to Resilient Retirement

In the spirit of continuous learning and adapting, I'm excited to offer you exclusive access to a **Free Resilience Course, a $197 value,** explicitly designed for transitioning retirees seeking to enhance their ability to bounce back from life's challenges and embrace the changes retirement brings. Please consider this course a personal workshop where you can further hone the skills discussed in our resilience chapter but with a focus tailored to your unique experiences and aspirations.

This course is structured around interactive modules that blend insightful, interactive content, reflective exercises, and actionable advice. Each module builds on the next, allowing you to develop a deeper understanding of resilience as it applies to unexpected setbacks and everyday retirement living. You'll learn to recognize the early signs of stress and anxiety, strategies to manage them, and ways to turn challenging situations into opportunities for growth and happiness.

One particularly beneficial aspect of the course is its community feature. Here, you can connect with other retirees navigating their post-career phases. This community provides a supportive environment where you can share experiences, offer advice, and receive encouragement. It's a place to remind you that you're not alone on this path and that your experiences are valid and valuable.

- To enroll in this FREE course, follow this link: **https://bit.ly/3U5blBp**.

Registration is straightforward; you can start the course quickly, fitting in with your existing schedule and commitments. Whether early in the morning with a cup of coffee or as a reflective end to your day, this course is designed to seamlessly integrate into your life, enhancing your journey to a resilient retirement.

Visualization and Mindfulness: A Sneak Peek into the Course Content

One module I'd like to highlight focuses on the power of visualization and mindfulness—techniques that foster a calm, positive mindset. Through guided sessions, you'll learn to visualize your ideal retirement lifestyle, defining what happiness and success mean to you now. These exercises not only promote mental clarity but also help in setting realistic, achievable goals.

Moreover, the mindfulness practices included in the course are tailored to help you cultivate a deeper appreciation for the present moment. This is especially beneficial for those worrying about the future or lamenting over the past. By bringing your focus to the here and now, mindfulness can significantly enhance your emotional well-being, making every day of retirement more joyful and fulfilling.

Engaging in this course will equip you with valuable skills and inspire a proactive approach to building and maintaining resilience. It's about more than just coping; it's about thriving. And with each step, you'll find yourself more adept at navigating the complexities and joys of retirement, armed with knowledge, strategies, and a supportive community.

As you continue exploring the various resources and opportunities outlined in this chapter, remember that each tool and insight is designed to enhance your journey, providing clarity and support as you explore the many facets of retirement. Whether through learning new resilience techniques, connecting with peers, or simply finding joy in daily activities, these resources facilitate a retirement as enriching and fulfilling as possible.

6.2 THIRTY DAYS FREE MFPA VAULT ACCESS

Navigating the financial landscape of retirement can often feel like trying to find your way through a labyrinth; with so many paths and directions, the sheer amount of information can be overwhelming. That's precisely why I've introduced the MFPA Vault, a cutting-edge platform designed to simplify your financial management. Think of it as your financial command center, where every significant piece of information is secured and easily accessible, allowing you to oversee your financial landscape with clarity and confidence.

The MFPA Vault, powered by RightCapital software, stands out for its robust security measures and comprehensive functionality. It uses bank-level security to protect financial data with the highest encryption and security protocol standards. This is the same level of security entrusted by Certified Financial Planner ® professionals, which means your information is as safeguarded as it would be in a financial institution. What makes this tool particularly appealing is its affordability; for less than $1 per day, you have access to a suite of tools that can transform how you manage your finances.

Imagine having the ability to integrate all your financial accounts in one place—from your savings and checking accounts to investments and retirement funds. The MFPA Vault does just that, providing a real-time overview of your financial status. This integration allows you to track your spending, monitor investment performance, and see your financial growth over time. It simplifies the often tedious task of keeping tabs on various accounts, making financial oversight easier and more effective.

Moreover, the platform includes budgeting, estate planning, and risk management tools tailored to retirees' needs. These tools help you create detailed financial plans, including scenarios for different spending levels and unexpected expenses, ensuring you can adjust your strategies as needed. For instance, The estate planning feature helps you manage your assets in a way that aligns with your future goals and legacy plans, providing peace of mind that your financial wishes are documented and manageable.

For those who might feel daunted by the prospect of using new technology, the MFPA Vault is designed with user-friendliness in mind. Its interface is intuitive, making navigation easy for all users. Additionally, numerous resources and support are available within the platform, including tutorial videos, to maximize the platform's benefits without frustration.

- To access the MFPA Vault, visit **https://mfpafp.com/products/.**

Scroll down the product page and Click MFPA Vault on the left.

You can try it FREE for 30 days. After that, it's less than $1 per day. You can cancel at any time.

Once you register, I will send you an access email, and then you can start linking your accounts and exploring the various features at your leisure. The initial setup is straightforward, and you are guided through each step with clear instructions, making it easy to get started even if you're not tech-savvy.

Remember, effective financial management in retirement is not just about keeping track of expenses or investments; it's about creating a sustainable strategy that supports your lifestyle and goals. With the MFPA Vault, you have a powerful tool at your fingertips that enhances your ability to manage your finances with precision and foresight. It's about taking proactive steps towards a secure financial future, ensuring you can enjoy your retirement with the peace of mind of a well-organized financial plan.

6.3 TWENTY EXTRA INCOME IDEAS FOR RETIREMENT

Discovering avenues for extra income in retirement isn't just about bolstering your financial security—it's also an enriching way to engage your skills, pass on your wisdom, and perhaps even explore passions that your working years left little time to pursue. Recognizing this, I've compiled a resource list that will be invaluable in your quest for meaningful and rewarding ways to enhance your retirement income. This guide, **20 Ways to Earn Extra Income in Retirement**, is designed to inspire and equip you with practical ideas tailored to your unique skills and interests.

You might wonder why a retired individual would want to look into earning additional income. Let me share a perspective that goes beyond the mere financial aspect. Engaging in work that resonates with your passions and strengths can bring a renewed sense of purpose and fulfillment. It keeps your mind active, skills sharp, and social networks vibrant. Whether consulting in your expert field, turning a hobby into a small business, or sharing your life experiences and knowledge through blogging or teaching, each opportunity can enrich your life in more ways than one.

For instance, consulting is a fantastic way to leverage your decades of professional experience. Many businesses seek seasoned experts who can offer insights and guidance without a long-term commitment. This allows you to work flexibly and engage meaningfully with your field of expertise, keeping you connected to the industry you love. On the other hand, if you're crafty, platforms like Etsy provide a global marketplace to sell your creations. This can be incredibly fulfilling, turning a leisure activity you love into a profitable venture, all from the comfort of your home.

Moreover, the internet offers unprecedented opportunities to create content based on your life experiences or professional knowledge. Starting a blog or a YouTube channel can be a delightful way to share your knowledge and stories with the world and earn revenue through advertising, sponsorships, or memberships. This type of work can be incredibly gratifying as it provides an income stream and allows you to connect with like-minded individuals globally, expanding your social circle and influence.

This guide describes each income idea and links to four or five examples. Whether you're looking to cover some extra expenses each month or fund new adventures, there's something in this guide for everyone.

- To access this FREE Guide, go to: **https://bit.ly/3SsfFcD**.

The guide is entirely free and available for download. It's PDF formatted for easy reading and can be accessed on any device, making it convenient for you to refer back to whenever inspiration strikes or when you're ready to take a step toward a new project.

As you explore these possibilities, remember that the goal is to earn money and enrich your life with meaningful activities that resonate with your passions and values. Each opportunity is more than a revenue stream; it's a chance to learn new skills, meet new people, and make a difference in your community or even globally. The world of retirement is evolving, and so are the opportunities within it. With the right resources and a proactive approach, you can craft a retirement that is as financially rewarding as it is personally fulfilling.

6.4 FREE BUDGETING TOOLS

Navigating the financial aspects of retirement can often feel like steering a ship through unfamiliar waters. With the right tools, however, you can chart a course that keeps you on track and enhances your financial confidence and control. This is where a practical budgeting tool comes into play, acting as your compass and map in managing your finances efficiently.

Understanding the importance of a well-structured budget, I've curated a budgeting tool specifically designed for retirees. This tool is available in PDF and Excel, so you can choose the format that best suits your comfort level and tech proficiency. The beauty of this tool lies in its simplicity and functionality. It is designed to help you easily create, track, and adjust your budget, helping you maintain a solid grasp of your financial health.

For instance, the Excel-based budgeting tool allows for automatic calculations and can be customized to include categories specific to your spending habits and income streams. Whether you're managing regular expenses, tracking investment incomes, or planning for occasional indulgences, this tool adapts to your life. It simplifies the often tedious process of adding expenses and forecasting monthly budgets, giving you more time to enjoy your retirement rather than managing numbers.

On the other hand, the PDF format provides a printable option that you can fill out manually. This can be particularly appealing if you prefer a hands-on approach or wish to keep a physical record of your financial planning. The PDF tool is structured to guide you through listing your income sources and expenses, helping you see where your money comes from and where it goes. This can be incredibly insightful, revealing patterns in your spending that you may want to adjust to align better with your retirement goals.

Both tools have examples already populated so that you can replace the information in the examples with your own.

To access these budgeting tools, enter the links below:

- Excel format tool at: **https://bit.ly/4fhZ4C5**.
- PDF format tool at: **https://bit.ly/46nDUyn**.

This will take you directly to the download page, where you can choose the format that best suits your needs. Once downloaded, you can integrate these tools into your financial routine immediately. Remember, using these tools keeps your finances in order and gives you a clearer, more comprehensive view of your financial landscape. This empowers you to make informed decisions that enhance your financial security and peace of mind.

6.5 FREE RISK ASSESSMENT TOOL

The University of Missouri offers a FREE tool to characterize your risk tolerance for certain investments. After completing the assessment questions, you will be placed in one of five risk tolerance categories. This information can be essential for your financial advisor or registered investment professional to ensure they are following your wishes and not putting you into investments that cause you to lose sleep and feel stressed.

- You can access the tool here: **https://bit.ly/46zjHpk.**

As we wrap up this chapter, we must reflect on the broader implications of the resources and tools provided. Each one, from resilience courses to financial vaults and budgeting tools, is designed to empower you with knowledge, simplify your life, and enhance your retirement experience. They are more than just tools; they are stepping stones to a retirement filled with confidence, security, and fulfillment. As you move forward, remember that these resources are here to support you in building a retirement that resonates with your dreams and aspirations. So, please take full advantage of them, tailor their use to your unique journey, and step confidently into the next chapter of your life, equipped with the tools and knowledge to thrive.

6.6 ADDITIONAL RESOURCES

- Check out https://www.retire.center for more tools and resources.
- Check out https://www.mfpafp.com for veteran resources.
- Check out https://www.maxretired.life for more joyful retirement information.

CONCLUSION

As we end our journey together within the pages of this book and close the curtains behind us for now, I'd like to pause and look back at the paths we've traveled side by side. We've delved into five impactful approaches to retirement: Extending Healthspan, Discovering Purpose, Crafting Memorable Moments, Fostering Resilience, and Securing Financial Stability. These strategies play a role, each adding its unique touch to weave a tapestry of happiness and fulfillment in our retired years.

Planning for retirement involves taking care of yourself physically and emotionally while securing your finances for the future, too! I've shared these strategies to help guide you through all aspects of post-work life.

It's crucial to emphasize the significance of planning in retirement preparation. By initiating your journey into retirement with defined and feasible strategies in place, you can significantly improve your quality of life, steer clear of typical regrets, and amplify your overall satisfaction. This book culminates in a lifetime filled with personal and professional encounters. Drawing from my background as a retired Major General with experience in military and corporate executive leadership roles and volunteer efforts to support veterans, I strive to offer practical and deeply insightful perspectives.

I urge you to incorporate these tactics sincerely and earnestly into your routine. Retirement isn't about your plans but the steps you take toward them. Your post-retirement days have the potential to be just as lively and rewarding as any life stage—even more so.

Feel free to dream big and start making choices for your retirement ahead! Whether rediscovering hobbies, strengthening bonds with loved ones, or venturing into new experiences, remember that chasing what makes you happy and fulfilled is always possible! Avoid living with regrets, as Bronnie Ware shares in her book *The Top Five Regrets of the Dying*.

Embrace the changing landscape of retirement with a mind and a willingness to learn and explore approaches and insights along the way! Just as life is a journey of evolution and adjustment, retirement is a path of growth and adaptation that benefits from sharing newfound wisdom with those around you—friends, family, and peers alike! By exchanging knowledge and experiences, you help build a community of informed retirees who lead fulfilling lives.

Thank you very much for taking the time to explore these pages with me! Your interest and openness to discussing retirement planning warms my heart and inspires me greatly. I'd be thrilled to hear about your experiences and obstacles that have shaped your retirement strategy using this book's insights and tools. Feel free to contact me via my website (https://mfpafp.com) or on social media for support and access to a supportive community of individuals sharing similar aspirations.

As we go our separate paths and bid farewell for now, remember that this is not the conclusion but rather a new commencement—a hopeful start to what I envision as the most delightful and rewarding chapters of your existence ahead of you! Here's to embracing the best of retired life—may it bring you all you have dreamt of and beyond. All the best,

- Pete Bosse, PhD, CFP®

REFERENCES

(2023). Switzerland: WHO outlines considerations for the regulation of artificial intelligence for health. MENA Report.

10 Passive Income Cash Flow Assets To Grow Wealth and Live Off Your Investments for Life - New Trader U. https://www.newtraderu.com/2023/06/29/10-passive-income-cash-flow-assets-to-grow-wealth-and-live-off-your-investments-for-life/

5 Ways To Keep Inflation From Wrecking Your Retirement https://www.bankrate.com/retirement/how-to-keep-inflation-from-wrecking-retirement/

7 High-Return, Low-Risk Investments for Retirees https://money.usnews.com/investing/articles/high-return-low-risk-investments-for-retirees

9 Ways to Boost Your Social Security Benefits - Investopedia https://www.investopedia.com/articles/retirement/112116/10-social-security-secrets-could-boost-your-benefits.asp

Anthony Bourdain: 'Eat at a Local Restaurant Tonight' Quote – Truth or Fiction? https://www.truthorfiction.com/anthony-bourdain-eat-at-a-local-restaurant-tonight-quote/

Better Technology, Better Retirement Savings https://www.aspeninstitute.org/events/better-technology-better-retirement-savings-why-operations-and-administrative-technology-matters-for-saver-outcomes/

Davis, J., Gibson, L., Bear, N., Finlay-Jones, A., Ohan, J., Silva, D., & Prescott, S. (2021). Can Positive Mindsets Be Protective Against Stress and Isolation Experienced during the COVID-19 Pandemic? A Mixed Methods Approach to Understanding Emotional Health and Wellbeing Needs of Perinatal Women. International Journal of Environmental Research and Public Health, 18(13), 6958.

Downsizing Your Home as You Retire - Market Business News. https://marketbusinessnews.com/downsizing-your-home-as-you-retire/259549/

Financial Fitness for the New Year: The Guide to Setting Your Q1 2024 Financial Goals - MVEMNT. https://www.mvemnt.com/financial-fitness-for-the-new-year-the-guide-to-setting-your-q1-2024-financial-goals/

Financial Freedom in Retirement: A Guide to Avoiding Credit Card Debt – Smartingly. https://smartingly.com/money/financial-freedom-in-retirement-a-guide-to-avoiding-credit-card-debt

Fogel, H. (2023). VAUGHAN WILLIAMS: Symphonies Nos. 61 and 92. The Wasps: Overture3. Fanfare, 46(3), 363-364.

Friebe, M., Friebe, M., & Illanes, A. (2023). Advancements in Medical Imaging and Image-Guided Procedures: A Potential—Or Rather Likely—Paradigm Shift in Diagnosis and Therapy: Understand Disruption and Take Advantage of It! Applied Sciences, 13(16), 9218.

Get started with Medicare https://www.medicare.gov/basics/get-started-with-medicare

Hidden Library Gems - The Quick Reads Collection. https://www.caldwellpubli clibrary.org/post/hidden-library-gems-the-qreads-collection

Holistic Health Approaches for Elderly Care https://friendshipcenters.org/holis tic-health-approaches-for-elderly-care/#:~:text=Holistic%20health%20ap proaches%20offer%20significant,and%20senior%20health%20and% 20wellness.

How a Charitable Trust Works https://smartasset.com/estate-planning/charitable-trust

How can cryptocurrencies be kept secure? - Crypto Mining Best. https://crypto mining.best/general/how-can-cryptocurrencies-be-kept-secure/70/

How do I avoid taxation when transferring my 401k? - Billyreedsays - 401k Gold IRA Financial. https://billyreedsays.com/how-do-i-avoid-taxation-when-trans ferring-my-401k/

How Retirement Changes Our Relationships https://georgejerjian.com/how-retire ment-changes-our-relationships/

How to Get Rich With a Normal Job. https://www.michpost.com/how-to-get-rich-with-normal-job/

How to Plan for Taxes in Retirement https://www.schwab.com/learn/story/how-to-plan-ahead-taxes-retirement

How to Prepare a Digital Estate Plan https://www.usbank.com/wealth-manage ment/financial-perspectives/trust-and-estate-planning/digital-estate-plan.html

How to save for retirement when you're in your 50s https://www.bankrate.com/ retirement/retirement-saving-tips-for-50s/

How Your Social Security May Be Taxed. https://www.imagine.biz/post/how-your-social-security-may-be-taxed

Investing for Income | Sterling Asset Management. https://www.sterling.com.jm/ blog/investing-income

Kafkaletou, M., Kalantzis, I., Karantzi, A. D., Christopoulos, M. V., & Tsantili, E. (2019). Phytochemical characterization in traditional and modern apricot (Prunus armeniaca L.) cultivars – Nutritional value and its relation to origin. Scientia Horticulturae. https://doi.org/10.1016/j.scienta.2019.04.032

Leaving a Lasting Legacy: A Scoping Review of Ethical Wills https://www.ncbi.nlm.nih.gov/pmc/articles/PMC9636071/

Loneliness and Social Isolation — Tips for Staying Connected https://www.nia.nih.gov/health/loneliness-and-social-isolation/loneliness-and-social-isolation-tips-staying-connected#:~

Long-term care insurance vs. self-funding: What's the right ... https://www.cbsnews.com/news/long-term-care-insurance-vs-self-funding-whats-the-right-choice-for-you/

Managing Chronic Conditions for Elderly Adults: The VNS ... https://www.ncbi.nlm.nih.gov/pmc/articles/PMC4194907/

Morse, H. (2024). 8 ESSENTIAL Skincare Routines. Alternative Medicine, (74), 34-35.

Navigating Intricacies of Social Security Spousal Benefits in Retirement: Maximizing Your Benefits - DR News - News, Retirement, Finance. https://drnewsemails.com/navigating-intricacies-of-social-security-spousal-benefits-in-retirement-maximizing-your-benefits/

Negotiating with Confidence: Key Strategies for Business Transactions in Idaho - Johnson May Law. https://www.johnsonmaylaw.com/blog/negotiating-confidence-key-strategies-business-transactions-idaho

Nurturing Our Girls: A Heartfelt Guide for Moms on Handling the Roller – Fancy Thoughts. https://myfancythoughts.com/blogs/news/nurturing-our-girls-a-heartfelt-guide-for-moms-on-handling-the-rollercoaster-of-teen-emotions

Psalm 90:12, the Living Bible (TLB)

Refinance Your Mortgage: Options and Benefits | Apache Mortgage. https://apachemortgage.com/refinance

Retiring Into a Recession? What You Need To Know https://www.cnbc.com/select/retiring-into-a-recession-what-you-need-to-know/

Retirement Calculator: How Much Do I Need to Retire? | InvestingAnswer. https://investinganswers.com/calculators/retirement

Robert Grimm, J. (2007). The Health Benefits of Volunteering: A Review of Recent Research. https://core.ac.uk/download/71340040.pdf

Singh, V., & Goyal, P. (2017). Ways of being happy: Discerning sources of happiness among young adults and adults. Indian Journal of Positive Psychology, 8(2), 208-213.

The 13 Best Ikigai Quotes. https://www.readthistwice.com/quotes/book/ikigai